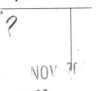

THE BOER WAR

South Africa 1899–1902

THE BOER WAR

South Africa 1899–1902

MARTIN MARIX EVANS

First published in Great Britain in 1999 by Osprey Publishing,
Elms Court, Chapel Way, Botley, Oxford OX2 9LP
E-mail: osprey@osprey-publishing.co.uk

ISBN 1 85532 851 8

Editor: Marcus Cowper
Design: Adrian Hodgkins Design
Typeset by: White Horse Graphics
Origination by Valhaven Ltd, Isleworth, UK
Printed through Worldprint, Hong Kong

99 00 01 02 03 10 9 8 7 6 5 4 3 2 1

For a catalogue of books published by Osprey Military please write to:

The Marketing Manager, Osprey Publishing Ltd., P O Box 140,
Wellingborough, Northants NN8 4ZA. UK
E-mail: info@OspreyDirect.co.uk

Osprey Direct USA, P O Box 130, Sterling Heights, MI 48311-0130,
USA
E-mail: info@OspreyDirectUSA.com

Or visit the Osprey website at: *http://www.osprey-publishing.co.uk*

Page 1 (half title) **Cape and Natal rebels of Bosman's
Commando** (McG MMKP797 8/17)

Page 2 (half title verso) **Biddulphsberg from the north. The
British attacked the hill from the right of this road and the
Ladybrand men occupied ditches to the left.** (MFME BW15/6)

Front Cover **Jan Smuts, centre, wearing a Sam Browne belt,
with his men in 1902. The youthful Deneys Reitz is kneeling,
bottom left.** (J. Deneys Reitz)

Back cover **The grave of Captain M. L. Hughes, RAMC, at
Clouston Cemetery. He was killed at Colenso on 15 December
1899, thus depriving his fellows of his continuing research
into perfecting a vaccine for typhoid.** (MFME BW16/23)

Endpapers **The Guards crossing the Modder River by way of
the dam at Rosmead.** (McGregor Museum, Kimberley)

ACKNOWLEDGEMENTS

The help and guidance given to me by people too numerous to list during my travels in South Africa was beyond price. In particular I thank Fiona Barbour and Brigit Carlstein of the McGregor Museum, Kimberley, Colonel F. J. Jacobs and Johan Hattingh of the War Museum of the Boer Republics, Bloemfontein, Pam McFadden of the Talana Museum, Dundee and Cornia de Villiers of the Ladysmith Siege Museum. Their patience with my questions and eagerness to assist in the enterprise has been invaluable. I owe Johan Hattingh a particular debt of gratitude for reading the draft manuscript and for his gentle guidance and suggestions for improvement. Doug McMaster not only gave generously of his time to show me the ground around Ladysmith, but also allowed me complete access to his huge collection of memorabilia, an act of hospitality and friendship most warmly appreciated. Ted Clouston led me to a fresh understanding and a startling view of Colenso. Pat Rendgren has been helpful in commenting on some of my conjectures. Gerhard Hattingh of Belmont and Frida van den Berg of Hopetown pointed me to places I would otherwise have missed. None of this would have been possible without the cheerful energy of Paul McIlvenny of Byeways and Battlefields, Scottsville, Pietermaritzburg, who arranged my journey and drove close on 3,000 miles to show me the scenes of battle and the archives that record the war.

In Britain there are also those to whom I owe special thanks: Colonel P. Worthy and George Durrant of the Museum of the Northamptonshire Regiment, Colonel J. E. Nowers and David Bryant of the Royal Engineers Museum and Maggie Lindsay Roxburgh of the Royal Engineers Library, and Thomas B. Smyth, Archivist of the Black Watch. The staff of the Bodleian Library, Oxford and the National Army Museum, London, have maintained their high standards of tolerance in the face of dim questioning. Bronwyn Fysh was particularly kind in sharing with me some conclusions of her work in progress on Lord Methuen. Lieutenant-Commander Brian Witts, MBE, of HMS *Excellent*, Portsmouth, gave me valuable guidance on the Royal Navy's contribution to the artillery actions of the war. Ken Vale, a fellow member of the Battlefields Trust, introduced me to some helpful references.

A NOTE ON THE TEXT AND MAPS

The subject of the Second Boer War is so large and the territory it covered so vast that much has been omitted here, and many of the places of which I write I have not visited. None of the Transvaal sites could be covered, and I have had to depend on secondary sources. As a result some queries in my own mind remain unresolved and the text reflects this. In making decisions about which actions are described I have favoured those that I know can be visited, have memorials or are provided with visitor facilities.

There seem to be a number of passionately-held but differing views on the spelling of place names. I have used the names I have found on current maps and signposts, and where there seem to me strong alternatives I have given both names, one in parens. Being unable to unlock the codes used by others, I have depended on what little common sense I possess and attempted to avoid confusing the reader. My apologies for any shortfall.

The war involved not only the English and the Boers, but the Scots, Irish and Welsh from the British Isles and the Australians, Canadians and New Zealanders from the British Empire; or, to be precise, those are the ones whose written records I have seen. In respect of the Australians I have relied on the work of R. L. Wallace, *The Australians at the Boer War*, and the Canadian experience is as recounted by Brian A. Reid in *Our Little Army in the Field*. The first hand reports of Australians and Canadians quoted in the text are drawn from these works, and the other quotations are taken from the books by the people quoted which are listed in the bibliography. The Australian quotes are Commonwealth of Australia copyright and are reproduced by permission of AusInfo. The passage from the letter of Private Williamson is reproduced by permission of the Trustees of the Black Watch Museum. The words of A. D. Bowers are reproduced by kind permission of his grandson, Simon May, and of Stephen Dance and the Editor of *Soldiers of the Queen* magazine. The substantial use of text from Deneys Reitz's *Commando* has been granted by his son, Jan Deneys Reitz, to whom I am very grateful. The Ladysmith Historical Society and Tuckwell Press have also been generous in allowing quotation from their publications. At the time of going to press the copyright owners of certain texts and illustrations have not been traced and the author would be grateful for information as to their identity and whereabouts.

Because maps were rare it has not been possible, with a very few exceptions, to reproduce the maps available to the commanders at the time. I have attempted, with some small success, to find such maps, but for the most part the cartography is all after the event. In some cases the map was made a matter of weeks after a battle, and is based on surveys of the site. In other cases, in an attempt to assist the reader, a later map, even a diagram, is offered to aid understanding of what happened, even if it does not reveal what the people present thought was going to happen. Lord Methuen's annotated map of the Modder River Crossing is the property of the Trustees of the Corsham Estate and I am grateful to James Methuen-Campbell for permission to use it.

NOTE ON THE ILLUSTRATIONS

The sources of the historical illustrations are noted in the captions, using, where it is known, the reference or accession number of the archive from which it comes. My photographs are annotated MFME/BW with the frame reference number, and include images from archives which I have been permitted, for the purposes of this work, to copy. The sources are identified by a name in full or the following abbreviations: BL = Bodleian Library, Oxford. LSM = Ladysmith Siege Museum, Ladysmith. McG = McGregor Museum, Kimberley. McM = Doug McMaster Collection, Ladysmith. NAM = National Army Museum, London. NRA = Northamptonshire Regiment Archive, Northampton. RE = Royal Engineers Library and Museum, Chatham. TM = Talana Museum, Dundee. The modern colour photography is mine with the exception of those marked M&CF which were kindly made available to me by Michael and Carol French and the Doornbult concentration camp cemetery picture which is reproduced by kind permission of Mrs Rina Wiid, Doornbult, Orange River, Hopetown 8751. Graham Jacobsen of The Bookcase, Sabie, generously gave permission for me to reproduce the pictures of documents noted as coming from his collection.

CONTENTS

THE BOER REPUBLICS

In October 1899 Britain, and thus the British Empire, went to war with the Boer Republics of the Transvaal and the Orange Free State. The state of war was precipitated by a Boer ultimatum that the British could not, and were not expected to, accept. It was a surprise to no one. The conflict between the settlers of Dutch origin and the British had its roots in events more than a century old.

The first Dutch arrived in the Cape in 1652 to create a base for the ships of the Dutch East India Company and a source of supply of fresh food for their crews. Jan van Riebeeck, with three small ships, arrived on 6 April to set up a fort, establish gardens for vegetables and seek good relations with the indigenous population, the Khoikhoi, from whom cattle were to be bought. The mission was not helped by the objections the Khoikhoi made to having their grazing lands taken for raising crops and the Dutch were obliged to explain that they had acquired the land by right of conquest, the first of many. The settlement was deliberately isolated from the rest of Africa and the attempt was made to dedicate it solely to meeting the needs of the Company; indeed, it was seriously proposed to dig a kind of moat to cut off the peninsula between False Bay and Table Bay. The idea was only rejected on grounds of expense. Neither isolation nor the plan of running the place with paid employees

worked. Settlers were needed to develop horticulture and they had objectives other than the service of the Company alone. The conflict between Company and settlers continued until the reforming Simon van der Stel arrived in 1679 and encouraged the development of a vigorous agricultural and forestry industry. The population of settlers achieved greater growth than intermarriage with the Khoikhoi could achieve when fleeing French Huguenots arrived after 1685. Their integration with the Dutch population fed the growth of a Calvinist society that saw itself as the chosen people of the Lord, entering into the Promised Land.

As the population grew, the pressures increased for the expansion of the territory controlled by Europeans and as the consequent migration took place conflict with the San, the hunter-gatherers of the interior, was inevitable. The commando was created to combat the resistance of the San to white expansion. All white men of sixteen years and over were registered and obliged to serve, without pay, under officers of their own choosing. Each man provided his own rations and horse, and the government furnished the weapons and ammunition. The methods developed in this warfare were to serve well in fighting against other black adversaries and equally against other whites. Thomas Pringle, journalist, reported a Boer commando expedition to destroy a San community, of which, when the firing ceased, only five women were found living. Four of these were killed when they failed to keep up with the homeward-bound commando, the lone survivor 'could by no means be torn from one of our comrades, whom she had grasped in her agony…' and so was suffered to live. By the end of the eighteenth century steps were being taken to protect the remaining San as an endangered species. In the meantime the Khoikhoi had also ceased to exist in their original, clan-based society, having been deprived of lands and cattle in warfare, decimated by smallpox and dispersed into a fragmented working class in the service of the settlers.

Slaves existed from the earliest days, imported from East Africa, Madagascar or from the Dutch East Indies by the Company. As time passed and as their number increased, the relatively liberal regulations gave way to more severe restrictions, though breaking at the wheel and slow strangulation were abolished as

Below **The colours of the 58th, carried at Laing's Nek, with, left to right, Colour-Sergeant Bridgestock, DCM, Private Osborne, VC, and Private Godfrey, DCM. All wear the Zulu War medal as well.**
(NRA. MFME BW17/34)

Above **The battlefield of Majuba Hill was a tourist destination for the 2nd Northamptonshire Regiment which had fought there in the first war. Major G. N. M. Darwell took a picture of the marker showing where General Sir George Colley fell.**
(NRA. MFME BW18/2)

Right **A Boer Voortrekker of the 1830s. He carries a double-barrelled flintlock and a powderhorn on a waistbelt.**
(Gerry Embleton, from Men-at-Arms 301 *Boer Wars (1) 1836–1898*)

punishments in 1799. At that time, in Cape Colony, there were more slaves than white people, and slave labour provided the greater part of the labour force.

The economy of the Cape collapsed in 1794 with the bankruptcy of the Dutch East India Company. By that time the main enemy appeared to be the Xhosa beyond the Fish River. But a year later a British flotilla dropped anchor in Simon's Bay, ostensibly to safeguard the colony from the French during hostilities and undertaking to return it to the Dutch as indeed, under the Treaty of Amiens, they did in February 1803. The peace was short-lived. As Napoleon threatened to exclude Britain from European and international commerce, Cape Town was vital to survival. Britain was back in 1806 and the occupation was made permanent at the Congress of Vienna at the end of the war. The British part of the population grew with, for example, the settlement of 1820 when some 5,000 were brought in to occupy farmland along the Fish River. The abolition of slavery in 1834 and such measures as the restriction of the language of courts of law to English, combined with the increasing shortage of land, persuaded the Dutch to seek their fortunes further north and east, so under such leaders as Piet Retief and Piet Uys, they trekked. In the decade from 1836 some 14,000 people, one sixth of the white population, left Cape Colony. With their herds of cattle and goats, their families and furniture in great ox-drawn wagons, their black servants following, and at a pace of some five miles a day, they crept across the land towards the High Veldt, towards the Orange and Vaal Rivers and beyond. Another chosen people in search of their Promised Land.

Their movement did not go unresisted. Hendrick Potgieter did battle with the Ndebele and, after Piet Retief's death with some 70 followers at the hands of Dingane's Zulu warriors, Andries Pretorius led a revenging commando of 500 men to a crushing victory at Blood River on 16 December 1837, killing 1,000 Zulus for each of the three Voortrekkers injured that day.

While the Afrikaners expanded inland, the British took control of the coast. Port Elizabeth grew with the eastward expansion of the Cape and Port Natal grew to become Durban after the annexation of the territory by the British in 1845. The Voortrekkers did not take kindly to being ruled, neither by the British nor by their own men, but slowly a state emerged to be recognised as the Transvaal in the Sand River Convention of 1852. Britain recognised its independence on condition that slavery was outlawed. The Bloemfontein Convention did the same for the Orange Free State in 1854. Two land-locked Boer entities now existed, comprised of five republics, three forming Transvaal (becoming the South African Republic in 1860), and two the Orange Free State. In

addition to being land-locked, they were isolated culturally, this isolation being reinforced by a strict Calvinist religious ethos. These states existed in a fluctuating state of conflict, both amongst themselves and with the surrounding black African territories.

Into this instability a new irritant thrust itself in 1867. On the banks of the Orange River at Hopetown a pretty stone was found, a diamond of 21.25 carats. The diamond fields of South Africa were to become the largest in the world. Two years later the vast resources of Kimberley were discovered in disputed territory which eventually became part of the Cape under the Keate Award of 1871, subsequently proven

to be ill-founded if not actually cooked up. Although compensation of £90,000 was paid to the deprived Orange Free State an additional cause for resentment had been given to the Boers. By 1871 there were more than 15,000 whites in the diamond fields, and by 1895 a half a million black people, one fifth labourers, the rest their dependants, had moved to the area. Many of these left their jobs with the Boers for the better paid, though still miserable, employment to be had in the minefields. Here too was Cecil John Rhodes, from Bishop's Stortford in Hertfordshire, to make his first £5,000 and start his career as a mining magnate.

The policy of the British was curiously muddled. On the one hand a stable environment was desired for the growing commercial wealth of Cape Colony and of Natal, to which the first group of indentured

Above **Francis William Reitz, Deneys Reitz's father, photographed during his tenure as President of the Orange Free State, 1880.** (J. Deneys Reitz)

Above right **The 58th Regiment was the last to carry its colours into battle, at Laing's Nek, below Majuba. The 2nd Northamptons, as the 58th had become, visited the monument to their fallen comrades.** (NRA. MFME BW18/8)

Right **President Kruger on the stoep, the porch, of his house in Pretoria.** (McM. MFME BW12/6)

labourers were brought from India in 1860 to meet a lack of manpower. At the same time expense was to be avoided, particularly the cost of sending troops. Even so the British fought a series of wars against the Xhosa. The apparent inability of the Transvaal to deal with growing black African threats offered a chance to the British to take over, which, with one emissary and 25 military police, they did in January 1877, and the South Africa Act later that year made the whole region subject to the Crown. This made the Zulu, formerly allies, into enemies and Cetshwayo's troops massacred a British force at Isandhlwana and were narrowly repulsed at Rorke's Drift in 1879, only, in the end, to suffer defeat at Ulundi.

The quiescence with which the Boers apparently accepted annexation was misleading. With the failure of two missions to negotiate independence, their leader, Paul Kruger, joined with Marthinus Pretorius and Piet Joubert to fight the First War of Independence. Victories at Bronkhorst Spruit, Majuba and Laing's Nek coupled with British reluctance to reinforce their investment in South Africa granted the Boers their wish, subject to foreign policy control by the British. But irrevocable damage had by now been done. Any spirit of trust had been

destroyed, and while personal enmity might not exist between individual Briton and Boer, the latter were more united than ever before and guided by deep distrust of people more interested in commerce than care of the soil and, worse, neglectful of the God-given status of white people as supreme.

The British were less concerned with the Boers than with other European nations and their interest in acquiring African colonies. French, German and Belgian territories joined the long-established Portuguese as Africa was carved up into lumps of European invention. The Berlin Convention of 1884 confirmed what force and guile had acquired. Germany's presence in south-west Africa was seen, given the apparent affinity of their peoples, as a step to alliance with the Afrikaners against the British, who, in their turn, worried the others with their vision of a Cape to Cairo railway and a conviction of the noble nature of imperialism – as long as it was British imperialism.

Any hope of stability was destroyed by the discovery of gold in the Witwatersrand, in Transvaal, in 1886. Although gold had been found in the northwest of the republic 20 years earlier, the massive fields available for exploitation called for huge investment. The ore in the sloping reefs required complex industrial processes to extract the gold itself, an undertaking that depended on finance by the rich diamond companies and on the supply of coal to fuel rail transport. The coal was to be found in northern Natal, in such places as Dundee and Elandslaagte, to be moved up to Johannesburg by rail. The final ingredient was cheap labour, easy to get by paying the Boer's workers a modicum more.

The economic impact of the goldfields in the next decade was vast. From near bankruptcy, Transvaal became awash with funds from tariffs and taxes. The dependence on the British for access to the sea was mitigated by the building of a railway to the Portuguese port at Delagoa Bay and in 1895 an

attempt was made by President Kruger to put the Cape railway out of business by closing the Vaal crossings. Cecil Rhodes successfully engaged the support of the Colonial Secretary, Joseph Chamberlain to issue threats sufficient to have them opened. The people who were creating this wealth, if the manual workers are put aside, had no voice in the use of it. The incomers, *uitlanders*, were not permitted the vote until they had a residence qualification of 14 years. As Sir Alfred Milner was to remark, 'Two antagonistic systems, a medieval race oligarchy and a modern industrial state' could not hope to exist side by side, especially when the former sought to rule the latter.

The first attempt to resolve the difficulty was made by Rhodes who fomented a coup. Dr Jameson, with 500 Rhodesian police, rode for Johannesburg expecting to support an uprising. The uitlanders did not rise up, and Jameson and his men suffered a humiliating surrender at Doornkop in January 1896. The fiasco finished Rhodes politically and he was obliged to resign as Cape Premier. Kruger himself was much strengthened as leader of the Afrikaner interest both in the Transvaal and throughout South Africa. An accord for mutual support was made with President Steyn of the Orange Free State the following year. In Europe the Kaiser, William II, offended public opinion in Britain by sending a message of congratulation to Kruger and thus strengthened support for imperialist policy and turned Jameson into a popular hero.

Joseph Chamberlain, having kept himself clear of direct involvement in the political mess created by Rhodes, pursued his imperial aims by appointing Sir Alfred Milner High Commissioner. Milner was subtle but determined to achieve British domination of the Boer republics. A secret treaty was made with Germany to deny the Transvaal control of the eastern route to the sea should Portugal cease to hold the territory and Milner then concentrated his energies on drawn-out negotiations with Kruger about the situation of the uitlanders. The uitlanders were not without reasonable cause in resenting Kruger's government. Their businesses were subject to heavy taxation, the English language was excluded from the law courts and education, the courts themselves were composed entirely of Afrikaner judges and juries and they were denied any political voice - much like the injustices from which the Voortrekkers had absented themselves in 1836. A supreme attempt was made by moderate Afrikaners to reach agreement at a conference in Bloemfontein early in 1899, but it stuck on the British attempt to assert supremacy over a self-governing Transvaal. Kruger and his State Secretary, F. W. Reitz, refused to surrender sovereignty.

Meanwhile the British were taking belated steps to build up their military presence. When Milner arrived on the scene, with a prospect of about 50,000 Boers taking to arms if it came to war, there were only some 10,000 British troops throughout the territory. Plans to double their number were resisted by the Secretary of State for War, Lord Lansdowne who agreed with the new GOC in Natal, Major-general Sir Penn Symons, that 5,000 would suffice. Milner put pressure on for more, and on 17 September 1899 10,000 men from the Mediterranean and Indian theatres began the move to Natal. Kruger's ultimatum was less than a month away.

TO WAGE A WAR

In Pretoria fourteen-year-old Freda Schlosberg was at school, Loreto Convent, on 27 September 1899. Rumours had been circulating for weeks past as the crisis deepened. Early in the day she was walking in the garden when:

'...I saw several horsemen with rifles galloping along the street and I guessed something had happened ... if war does break out we shall be free from lessons, and that in itself would be a great blessing. Then the day-scholars arrive and bring the news that the burghers have been mobilised and are to leave for the front immediately, and that war has been declared.

'In the afternoon some of us are allowed to go into town with Sister Ursula. The streets are crowded. Boers on horseback, equipped with rifles, bandoliers, etc., are converging towards Government Buildings to hear General Joubert, the Commandant-general, make a long and eloquent speech. Afterwards the men proceed to the railway station. By four o'clock 4,000 Boers have left Pretoria for the Natal border.'

A few days earlier Deneys Reitz, the seventeen-year-old son of Secretary of State F. W. Reitz, had accompanied his father on a visit to President Kruger. The President told him:

'Piet Joubert says the English are three to one – Sal jij mij drie rooi-nekke lever?' (Will you stand me good for three of them?)'

Young Deneys undertook to do so, and when Kruger discovered he was thought too young to serve,

took him straight to Joubert to be enrolled. When the Pretoria men were mobilised (Reitz says it was on 29 September):

'... The moment we heard of this [mobilisation] we took our rifles, fetched our horses from the stable, and within minutes had saddled up and mounted.'

Reitz and his brother Joubert, named after the General, went into town to bid their father farewell and found he was in conference with the President and the Executive Council. Nonetheless they went in, said they had come to say goodbye and everyone present rose to shake their hands. Then they went to the station, loaded their animals and gave a hand with shifting stores and ammunition.

'As for my brother and myself, we were not Transvaal burghers, nor had we been called out for service, but we automatically became soldiers of the Boer Army by virtue of having thrown our belongings through a carriage window and clambering aboard, little knowing on how long and difficult a trail this light-hearted enlistment was starting us.'

PREPARATIONS FOR WAR

The romantic vision of a bunch of Boers saddling up and riding off to war with minimal preparation is misleading. Ever since revenues from the gold business had started fattening the coffers of the Transvaal government, and the Jameson Raid had shown Kruger how poorly armed his country was, the purchase of arms had been a major expense. Nor were the forces entirely militia. The Transvaal's regular soldiers were now some 600 Staats Artillerie, mainly German-trained gunners, and 1,400 state police, the Zuid-Afrikaansche Republiek Politie, known as the ZARP. The Orange Free State had about 400 gunners and the two republics had some 75 modern guns between them.

The guns themselves were mostly state-of-the-art. The majority were 75mm Creusot or Krupp pieces with a range of 8,500 yards (4.83m/7.77km) firing a high explosive fragmentation shell of 14.5lb/6.58kg. The design of the shell was less than perfect as it had an internal surface curved into sections about 3cm/1.25in. wide which resulted in the missile breaking up into quite large fragments when it exploded, thus reducing its chances of hitting someone. Anyone hit would be severely wounded or killed, but the object of the exercise is to wound sufficiently to incapacitate the enemy for the time

Below **Men of the Staats Artillerie in their field uniforms with a howitzer outside Ladysmith.** (McM. MFME BW12/4)

Left **The Hollander Commando leaving Pretoria on 6 October, 1899. Foreigners came from Europe, Russia and the USA to support the Boers, although some did little more than talk and live at their hosts' expense.** (McG. MMKP 3428)

Below **A British pom-pom. The performance of these guns in the hands of the Boers convinced the British that they should be using them as well. In later wars they were used against thin-skinned transports, ships and aircraft.** (NRA. MFME BW18/5.)

Bottom left **A replica Creusot on display at the War Museum of the Boer Republics, Bloemfontein.** (MFME BW15/1)

being and thus neutralise at least two fit comrades to assist the victim; three for the price of one. The Staats Artillerie had four 155mm Creusots, *Long Toms*, capable of hurling an 88lb/39.9kg high explosive shell more than 6 miles (10km), a formidable weapon that the Boers contrived to take into positions more remote and difficult to access than most could imagine. There were also four 120mm howitzers from Krupp. The Creusots came from France and the Krupps from Germany. Britain also supplied the republics – with the experimental Maxim-Nordenfeldt 1-pdr. machine-gun, the 'pom-pom'. This had a range of only 3,000 yards (1.7m/2.74km) and threw a little shell of 37mm calibre intended to explode on impact. It often failed to do so. However, if hit by one, the victim suffered terrible wounds, but if the shell exploded in the

ground it was virtually neutralised and if in the air fragmented inefficiently. The gun was, nonetheless, feared partly because of the speed of fire and partly because it could be taken into places into which other artillery could not go. By the end of the war the British were using them as well. With less modern guns the total strength approached 100 pieces. The Boers also had 30 Maxim-Vickers machine-guns, the precursors of the famous weapon of the First World War, mounted on light carriages.

Perhaps the most crucial decision was to arm the men of the commandos or to sell them new rifles at low prices. Traditionally they brought their own weapons and were to be provided with ammunition. When the matter was investigated in the aftermath of the Jameson Raid, it was discovered that forty per cent of Transvaal burghers had no rifle at all and that many of the rest only had ancient weapons, some of them

flintlocks. A large consignment, 10,450 single-shot 0.577-450in. 'improved' Martini-Henry rifles and 2,000 carbines had been acquired from Westley Richards of Birmingham. Notwithstanding the additional expense 37,000 German 7mm Mauser M1896s were purchased by Transvaal and 13,000 of them by the Orange Free State. These small-bore, high-velocity weapons used smokeless powder and were magazine loading. What was more, the magazine was reloaded by use of a clip, allowing it to be replenished with five cartridges in a single motion rather than filled up round by round. One characteristic of their performance was not fully appreciated until later in the war – the flat trajectory, similar to the Lee-Enfield of the British. Colonel W. F. Stevenson, who saw service in South Africa and became Professor of Military Surgery at the Royal Army Medical College, pointed out the advantage when firing at anything over point blank range.

'... Elevation must be given to the rifle ... [Thus] a bullet is only dangerous when it has again come sufficiently close to the ground ... when it has reached what is called the point of "first catch" on its trajectory. The point of "first catch" is, for cavalry, about 8½ feet [2.59m.] from the ground, and for infantry about 6 feet [1.83m]. The "dangerous zone" of a projectile is from the "first catch" to the end of its flight...'

He continues to explain that, the flatter the trajectory, the longer the dangerous zone and as this is achieved by having a higher muzzle velocity, that is,

the speed at which the bullet leaves the muzzle of the rifle, a number of other advantages accrue. First, the bullet is harder hitting and more destructive. Second, less elevation is needed in aiming, thus reducing the need for judgement and increasing accuracy. Third, the extent of point blank range is increased. Whereas the Martini-Henry has a point blank range of 400 yards (366m) the Lee-Enfield's is 500 yards (457m).

There were further influences resulting from these more modern weapons. The Martini-Henry used black powder as a propellant whereas the Boers' Mausers used smokeless powder. The British had considerable difficulty in pinpointing the source of rifle fire in these circumstances. The bullet itself had effects that were caused by its structure. In order to withstand the forces involved in thrusting a missile out of a rifled barrel at high velocity and to avoid an eroding bullet clogging the rifling, it was necessary to encase the largely leaden core in a cupro-nickel envelope. The bullet was therefore capable of shattering if the integrity of the casing was breached, either by hitting something like a bone, or by being compromised by cutting or abrasion. Both possibilities produced the effect of a 'dum-dum' bullet, though only in the latter circumstances intentionally. Moreover, the passage of a disintegrating bullet through flesh could lead to massive wounds that gave the impression of an exploding miniature shell. Stevenson himself was sure that the Boers did not, in spite of numerous

Right **This picture is captioned: Dutch Amazons at Newcastle, Natal, Dingaan's Day, 1900. It is probably a picture set up to accompany the one of the men, though some Boer women did fight alongside their men.** (McM. MFME BW11/3)

allegations to the contrary, ordinarily use explosive bullets. That some used dum-dums is undoubted, but it is likely that they were less than the evidence from wounds alone suggested.

In 1899 there were approximately 50,000 men available to the Boers. The commando system relied on the obligation of able, adult men to serve, each local district providing a contingent commanded by a *Veldt-kornet*. This unit might number anything between 150 and 200 men, and a number of them taken together constituted a commando. The smallest commando was Springs – 60 men. The largest was Potchefstroom with 3,000. Officers were elected by the men, and not always for their military prowess. Discipline and obedience were negotiable; an order considered foolish would simply not be obeyed. The tradition of the old farm-based, hunter-rifleman Trek-Boer had, by this time, been diluted by softer living and urbanisation, but the calibre in terms of marksmanship and horsemanship of those called to serve was still vastly greater than the average British recruit.

The Boers were not left to fight this war entirely alone, for the spectacle of a major power trying to cow two small republics into submission by threat of force brought men to their aid, either through a distaste for Britain or because of a devotion to the cause of freedom. An Irish Brigade was commanded by an American, Colonel J. Y. F. Blake, and European volunteers, including French, Italians and Russians, by the Frenchman Colonel Count Georges de Villebois-Mareuil. Not all of them came for the right reasons and their ideas of liberty and freedom usually excluded black people. A Frenchman from Villebois-Mareuil's unit told a Belgian nurse that it was an anti-Semitic war he had come to wage, the whole thing being a plot to obtain the gold of the Transvaal for Jewish bankers. The volunteers found it difficult to integrate with the Boer units, the lack of formal structure and curious attitude to discipline was hard for them to live with.

THE EMPIRE RALLIES

Although the Boers at the outbreak of war substantially outnumbered the forces available to Britain within South Africa, the long-term potential at the Empire's disposal in men, money and munitions was immense. What is more, the support for the British cause within the Empire was complete and, with supremacy at sea, the means of bringing the men to the conflict was available. By the end of the war Britain would have sent 358,000 men, including 18,000 Regulars from India, Australia would contribute 16,600, Canada 8,400 and New Zealand a surprisingly large number for a country of her size, 6,500 men. The heart of the British Army at the time was the infantry regiment and those responsible for raising forces from the Empire placed their confidence in raising more of the same. On 3 October 1899 Chamberlain cabled Canada to thank her for the offer of troops saying:

Above **A Boer commando at Newcastle, probably photographed at the same time as the 'Amazons', given the location. This picture later caused problems for a number of Boers who claimed they had taken no part in the war.** (McM. MFME BW11/9)

Below **The officers of the Irish Brigade at Ladysmith. The brigade was commanded by the American J. Y. F. Blake, seen here wearing a white jacket.** (McM. MFME BW11/10)

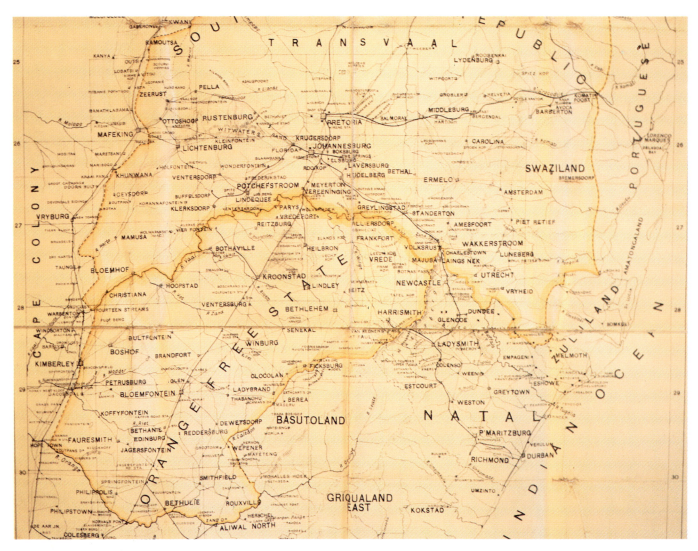

Above **Intelligence Division War Office map No. 1445, dated 1900. No such map was available to the troops in South Africa in 1899.**

(NRA. MFME BWMF11)

'Firstly, units should consist of about 125 men; secondly, may be infantry, mounted infantry, or cavalry; in view of numbers already available infantry most, cavalry least, serviceable …'

The Imperial Government was willing to furnish the .303 rifles or carbines, but the rest of the equipment and the horses for the mounted troops were to be provided by the colony or dominion, as was transportation to South Africa. The units were to serve 'for a term of six months, or one year if required, or until sooner lawfully discharged or dismissed…'

The first Australians to arrive were the New South Wales Lancers who had been in England at the outbreak of hostilities and 72 of them, under Captain C. F. Cox, left for South Africa in October. Later that month contingents from New South Wales, Queensland and Victoria embarked from Australia. On 30 October 2 (Special Service) Battalion, Royal Canadian Regiment of Infantry, which had been conjured into existence in a matter of weeks, sailed from Quebec. New Zealand's First Contingent of 214 officers and men left home on 21 October.

The British had taken the first steps to reinforce the troops in South Africa in September, though some token action was taken a little earlier when ten officers, including Lieutenant-colonels Robert Baden-Powell and Herbert Plumer, were sent out. Baden-Powell and Plumer raised small units in Rhodesia. On 22 September the British mobilised. An Army Corps of 47,000 men was to go, under General Sir Redvers Buller, V.C. In the event there were only 27,000 in South Africa at the outbreak of war, of whom some 8,500 were local volunteers such as the Natal Carbineers, the Imperial Light Horse and the Cape Mounted Police. The volunteer forces included numerous men from other parts of the Empire, for the goldfields had drawn experienced miners from Australia and Canada who had to leave by way of Kruger's railway eastwards to take passage from Delagoa Bay to Durban, there to join up.

Buller himself had been worried by his appointment, pointing out to Lord Lansdowne that he had never held independent command and that the circumstances, an expedition 6,000 miles from home, demanded skills perhaps best found by dividing the tasks between two people; perhaps the Commander-in-Chief of the British Army, Field marshal Lord Wolseley, would best be in overall command. The suggestion fell on deaf ears. Unfortunately Lansdowne was a weak member of the Government and presided over a divided army. The rival for the appointment now held by Wolseley was Field marshal Lord Roberts, who had been Commander-in-Chief in India when Lansdowne was Viceroy and with whom he had developed a good relationship. Wolseley had won distinction in campaigns in Africa. The army was thus divided between the Africans, of which Buller was one, and the Indians. The enmity of these two 'rings' was to poison the conduct of the war, but what was worse was the indecisive and procrastinating attitude of the key official, the Secretary for War himself. Buller had no staff to make preparations for the war that threatened throughout the English summer of 1899 and Lansdowne had no funds available to build the supplies that would be needed. In desperation Buller, in a memorandum dated 2 September, had told the Prime Minister, Lord Salisbury:

'We have, say, 13,000 men in South Africa … I estimate that to reinforce them we could get - 5,000 men from India in five weeks … 10,000 men from England in eleven weeks from date of order; an Army corps from England in sixteen to twenty weeks …

'Before we operate against the Boers we should know the line on which we are to advance, i.e., whether by the Orange Free State or by Natal… I have never yet had the route fixed, but I have gathered from Lord Lansdowne that he thinks the Natal route will prove the only possible one. Natal is a wedge 240 miles [386km.] deep, and for 100 miles [161 km.] of that depth the point of the wedge is bounded by a hostile country …'

Buller then set out the disposition of the 50,000 men he deemed necessary, and pointed out that an ultimatum to the Boers unsupported by appropriate strength would result in a Boer invasion. His final, sour conclusion:

'The situation is one in which the diplomatic authorities should consult with the military authorities.'

This direct approach to the Prime Minister did nothing for his relationship with Lansdowne.

To what extent anyone in England really understood the challenge of the terrain is difficult to establish. The preparation of maps was hampered by the lack of detailed surveys. Northern Natal had been surveyed from the South African Republic border south of Volksrust to an east-west line just north of Ladysmith and maps had been published by the Intelligence Division, War Office in April 1897. These maps were fairly reliable along existing roads and railways, but became vague away from recognised routes. The area south of Ladysmith, the hills along the Tugela River, had not yet been mapped or surveyed. In the Cape and the Orange Free State Captain W. A. J. O'Meara had been surveying since July, but the results of his work had yet to be seen in the form of a properly drawn map. There appears to have been absolutely nothing sufficiently detailed to permit the planning of an attack by a body of men fewer than 50. Schoolboy atlases or schoolroom wall maps were just about as good as you could get.

The broad shape of the country was, however, reasonably clear and the major rivers, mountain ranges, roads and railways known. The coastal plain is narrow and the land rises swiftly towards the vast interior plains of the High Veldt, at 6,500 feet (2,000m), separated from the south-eastern coast by the mountainous country of the Drakensburgs. The wealth of minerals at Kimberley and Johannesburg had led to the construction of railways from Cape Town to Kimberley and on to Mafeking and Rhodesia, from Port Elizabeth to Bloemfontein, Johannesburg, Pretoria and, in the far north, Pietersberg and from Durban to Ladysmith and north to Johannesburg. The eastwards connection from Pretoria to Delagoa Bay was newly completed. These lines had few cross-connections. The most important from the British point of view were the lines from De Aar on the Cape to Kimberley line to Naauwpoort on the Port Elizabeth to Bloemfontein line and on to Rosmead and Stormberg Junctions on the lines up from Port Alfred and East London. These were great distances. From Cape Town to Kimberley is some 650 miles (1,045km) and to Pretoria by rail is over 1,000 miles (1,600km). Durban to Ladysmith is about 190 rail miles (305km) and challenging miles they are, up through the tumble of hills that separate Pietermaritzburg from the sea and then on over high,

Below **Three men of the Natal Mounted Infantry at Ladysmith; left to right, Wilkins, Kemp and Fourier.** (McM MFME BW11/1)

rolling country before winding up the hills north of the Tugela to Ladysmith with still another 320 miles (500km) on to Pretoria. The climate offers hot summers with rain from October to March and cold, dry winters on the High Veldt, deserts to the west and maritime, almost British, conditions in the south east. Roads were, and many still are, packed dirt which turns into a slippery skid-patch when first wet then cuts up into a morass as cart wheels carve it up.

This short, generalised summary does small justice to the difficulty of the terrain for the movement of armies, their artillery, ammunition and supplies. The only routes available to the British for major troop movements were the railways. It is equally hard to convey to inhabitants of temperate climes such as Europe the quality of the terrain; the rocky soil and sparse, scrubby vegetation; the mesa-like kopjes, flat-topped, steep-sided hills; the spruits, dried river beds capable of turning into torrential death-traps after rain; the clarity of the air that gives a distant kopje the appearance of proximity. Of the soldiers going there only a few, those who had fought there before or some

of the Australians, had previously experienced anything of the kind.

Three days after leaving Pretoria Deneys Reitz and his brother reached Sandspruit, about ten miles from the Natal border.

'For the next ten days we lay here enjoying the novelty of our surroundings, as if we were on a pleasure jaunt, rather than seriously awaiting the coming of war. One evening my brother and I received a pleasant surprise, for there arrived in camp an old native servant of ours, grinning from ear to ear at having found us. His name was Charley … He was more than welcome for we could now turn over to him our cooking and the care of our horses …'

On 10 October they held a parade to celebrate Kruger's birthday and Piet Joubert announced that an ultimatum, written by Deneys's father, had been sent to the British. That night few slept as they sat round their camp fires, talking and singing, some until dawn. The next day five days' rations of biltong and meal were issued. The advance into Natal was to be made without the transport, so Charley was sent back to the

Below **The 1st Battalion, the Devonshire Regiment arrive in Ladysmith.** (TM. MFME BW4/15)

Right **A Boer woman posing
modestly in her bonnet. What
may be more significant is
the Martini rifle that can just
be made out on the original
print in the lower right of the
picture.** (McM. MFME BW16/6)

wagons and Deneys and Joubert prepared to ride with what they could carry.

Before noon on 12 October Reitz and his companions had reached Volksrust on the Natal border and spent the day and next night there before, in heavy rain, proceeding south. The invasion of Natal had begun.

On 14 October a huge crowd saw General Sir Redvers Buller board the *Dunottar Castle* on his way to South Africa. Six days later Second Lieutenant C. W. Barton recorded that the Headquarters and Right-half Battalion of his regiment, the 2nd Northamptonshire Regiment (formerly the 58th Foot) embarked at Southampton under the command of Lieutenant-colonel H. C. Denny and on 21 October Left-half Battalion under Major W. F. Fawcett was on its way from Aldershot.

'Great enthusiasm was displayed all along the line by all who saw the train full of troops. Men waving their hats, women their handkerchiefs & children flags; one patriotic old lady wearing a red coat & helmet mounting the railings of her house to give us the farewell wave of her hand…

'Great was the cheering & warm the send off of the crowd at Southampton docks, as well as the salute of the various vessels we passed as we slowly left the harbour. A cornet player giving us "The Cock of the North", "Soldiers of the Queen", etc., while a small steamer full of trippers kept alongside to see us out, the shilling sightseers crowding to the starboard side till the vessel heeled over, then they broke out in "Rule Britannia", the whistle screamed a last goodbye & turning round she headed back to the shore.

'The "Nubia" (P&O) that took us on board is certainly a most comfortable vessel fitted with all the latest luxuries. Electric light everywhere of course and more resembling a London hotel than a boat.'

On 29 September Freda Schlosberg had returned home to the farm at Bronkhorstspruit, where the British 94th Regiment had been ambushed in December 1880. 'The graves of these men are a little distance from our home,' she wrote, 'under the scorching sun, far away from their native land…' On the night of 30 September the family was awakened by Field Cornet Piet Uys seeking accommodation for his commando of 200 men.

'These young men are very arrogant and say that they will drive the English into the sea; and after that all uitlanders, who, they say, are intruders and not welcome. This saddens us, for we are uitlanders. When Mr Uys heard this talk he was very grave and filled with dark thoughts regarding the future of his country… At breakfast Mr Uys declared it would be a fierce and terrible war, and although he did not say it I could see he thought the Boers would be conquered.'

Freda's father had come to South Africa from the western border of Russia, and he and his family were,

in law, Russians. An advantage was that Freda's brothers did not have to serve. The disadvantage was their position as adherents to neither side in the conflict, suffering the suspicions of both.

Away to the west on the railway line to Rhodesia at Mafeking, Colonel Baden-Powell's force of some 1,200 men was besieged by 5,000 Boers under Piet Cronje and J. H. De la Rey. There were substantial stores in the town as a trader, Mr Ben Weil, who had his wholesale business headquarters there, had accepted an assurance from the British Prime Minister's son and Baden-Powell's second-in-command, Lord Edward Cecil, that they would be paid for. Downline to the south of Mafeking, on the border of the Cape and the Orange Free State, the route for relief from Cape Town was blocked on 14 October when Kimberley was besieged by about 7,000 men. Here Lieutenant-colonel R. G. Kekewich had 600 Regular soldiers, including his own regiment, the 1st Loyal North Lancashire, and some 2,000 police and volunteers. By happy or unhappy chance, depending on whose side you were on, Cecil Rhodes was in town at the time and had to remain there, making strident demands of his political friends to be rescued and behaving to Kekewich as if the military was a subsidiary of his business. North of Mafeking only a small force under Plumer was available, unable to move to the relief as it was vulnerable on the long flank with Transvaal territory. On the western front the situation stayed static. In Natal Joubert was on the move south, soon to be joined from the Orange Free State by Prinsloo. Meanwhile Buller was isolated and out of touch on the high seas.

BESIEGED!

Deneys Reitz summed up the situation at the outbreak of war: *'The two republics had mobilized between 60,000 and 70,000 horsemen, at this moment distributed west and east, ready to invade Cape Colony and Natal at the given word. This great force, armed with modern weapons, was a formidable fighting machine which, had it been better led, might have made far other history than it did.'*

For the time being the Boers had a massive advantage in numbers. They had arms and ammunition. It would clearly be some time before the British could assemble armies capable of ejecting them from Cape Colony and Natal. Their leaders, however, were the heroes of 1881, the men who had led them in the First War of Independence, and having crossed the borders of the British colonies, they seemed to have little idea what to do next, other than to sit and watch the towns they surrounded. In Natal, at any rate, they were still on the move.

The GOC in Natal appointed in July was Major-general Sir Penn Symons who was still in the colony in September when, in view of the reinforcements now being sent, Lansdowne appointed a member of Lord Roberts's 'Indian' Ring, the current Quartermaster-

General Lieutenant-general Sir George White, to be GOC the enlarged force in Natal. White chose for his staff two more Indians, Colonel Ian Hamilton and Lieutenant-colonel Henry Rawlinson. The defence of Natal was, naturally, of great concern to the Governor, Sir Walter Hely-Hutchinson. He encouraged Symons, and later White, to push well north, at least to protect Dundee, on the grounds that anything less would 'disgust' the people of Natal and could provoke an uprising both of Afrikaners and Zulus. It seems far more likely that the possession of the rich coal mining area was uppermost in the minds of the colonists, for the market in the Transvaal being closed to them, there were attractive possibilities for coaling the ships bringing troops to Durban. The soldiers were doubtless influenced by the fact that the only detailed mapping was of territory north of Ladysmith. Buller, on the other hand, feared the consequences of over-long supply lines and vulnerable little garrisons that could be outflanked and picked off by the invading Boers. He pressed Lansdowne to restrain White from pushing farther north than the Tugela River. Meanwhile Symons garrisoned Dundee and White moved up to Ladysmith to join

Below **Looking south-west towards the Biggarsberg range from the rock-strewn slopes of Talana Hill with the museum buildings below. The difficulty of assaulting a hill over such terrain and under fire must have been immense.** (MFME BW4/33)

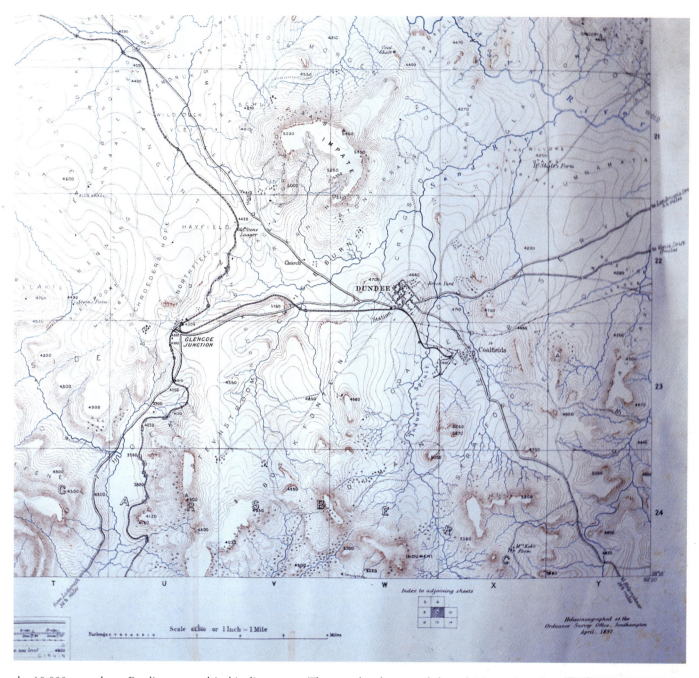

the 10,000 men there. Rawlinson noted in his diary that the sole military option was to withdraw to hold the Tugela line.

General 'Maroola' Erasmus's commandos were moving south. Reitz recounts:

'As soon as we were through the [Buffalo] river, we spread out on a front of several miles, and went forward. Far away, on either side, we could see the other forces moving abreast of us. There was not a man who did not believe that we were heading straight for the coast, and it was as well … that we did not know how our strength and enthusiasm were to be frittered away in a meaningless siege … when our only salvation lay in rapid advance.'

The next day they passed through Newcastle and then made a night march which brought them within 15 miles of Dundee.

TALANA

General Joubert briefed them for an another night advance in which Erasmus's troops would occupy the mountain overlooking the British camp, Impati, while the others would close around the flanks. It was a difficult march over muddy terrain, until at last, illuminated by lightning, the slopes were before them. Certain that the summit would be garrisoned, they climbed as silently as they might only to find themselves unopposed. There they waited in the rain

Above **Intelligence Division, War Office map No. 1223, sheet 9, April 1897. Entitled *Military Sketch of the Biggarsberg and of the Communications in Natal*, it was limited in scope. The southern portion has detailed contours, but things are pretty vague in the north-west. Dundee is in square W22 and Talana Hill lies north of the road in X22.** (TM. MFME BWMF2)

Right **Smith's Farm, below Talana Hill, from John Singleton's** *The Battlefields of Natal Revisited*, **published in Durban.** (TM. MFME BW3/33)

Below **The 1st King's Royal Rifles memorial and British graves, Talana, Dundee.** (MFME BW4/28)

until daybreak, and then waited some more in the fog. From somewhere to the south-east the sounds of battle thrust through the mist, but on Impati Erasmus had them stand still, waiting developments.

Lucas Meyer's commando occupied Talana Hill and Lennox Hill which stand north and south of the road east from Dundee towards Greytown. On Talana he positioned two 75mm Creusots and a pom-pom before daybreak. Their approach did not go entirely undetected as they ran into a piquet of Royal Dublin Fusiliers at about 3.20am, but after a few shots the Irishmen established themselves where the road crosses Sandspruit, between the hills and the town, and reported the incident. No one seemed to care much. After parade at 4.30 Lieutenant R. G. Stirling of 1st King's Royal Rifles was going to find a cup of tea when one of his fellows said: 'There they are!' Laughter faded as the first shells fell. Fortunately the sodden ground provided a gentle landing for the percussion

shells, many of which failed to explode.

Penn Symons had two batteries engage the Boer guns and sent the rest of the Royal Dublin Fusiliers to join their comrades in the donga, the dried-up bed of Sandspruit, with the 1st King's Royal Rifles and then the 1st Royal Irish Fusiliers following up. They faced, after a sloping approach through the grounds of Smith's farm, a wood and then a wall before the ground rose more steeply towards the Boer positions. The wall was crowned with a dense, prickly hedge and men filed riskily through a gate. Impatient at time lost, Penn Symons rode up, prominent with a red pennant carried by an orderly, and dismounted to chivvy the Rifles forward. He was shot and, attempting to conceal his fatal wound from his men, left the field. Colonel James Yule assumed command. Eventually, in the late morning, the infantry achieved the summit of the hill with a bayonet charge. Their officers had led from the front, the men had held formation at two-yard intervals and all had suffered fearfully as a result, 447 killed, wounded or missing. The Boers, as the British would soon become aware was their custom, had largely evacuated the summit of the hill before the final attack went in.

Meanwhile the fog had cleared and Reitz, looking back from the top of Impati, saw a body of horsemen to the rear. It was Lieutenant-colonel Möller with 300 men of the 18th Hussars. He had been told to use his discretion in moving to cut off the Boers retreating from Talana, but now found himself exposed to attack by 1,500 of them. Reitz reports:

'... *There were only a few of us saw the troopers on the plain behind...we mounted our horses and rode down the mountain-side as fast as we could go... The English had gone to earth at a small homestead, and we were just in time to see soldiers jumping from their horses, and running for cover to the walls of a stone cattle kraal, and among the rocks behind the farmhouse... Now, for the*

Left **Smith's Farm and British graves, in the grounds of the Talana Museum, Dundee.** (MFME BW 4/36)

Below **Singleton's picture of the kopje at Elandslaagte, taken soon after the war.** (TM. MFME BW3.31)

first time in my life, I heard the sharp hiss of rifle-bullets about my ears… My previous ideas of a battle had been different, for there was almost nothing to see here. The soldiers were hidden, and, except for an occasional helmet and the spurts of dust flicked up around us, there was nothing.

'… By now the countryside was buzzing like an angry hive, with men arriving from every direction, and the end was but a question of time. After a few minutes a Creusot gun of the Transvaal Staats Artillerie unlimbered and opened fire. The very first shell stampeded all the troop horses… I saw a white flag go up at the kraal, and another from the farmhouse …'

Reitz was disappointed to see that the English were dressed in khaki instead of scarlet uniforms, interested to note that, while the commanding officer was downcast, the men seemed much more cheerful and shocked to find that the dead had none of the dignity of death in battle he had expected, the 'ashen faces and staring eyeballs' were 'horrible to look upon'. Erasmus withdrew from Impati the next day, but the Boers then managed to haul one of their Creusots up the mountain and started lobbing shells through the rain into Dundee.

ELANDSLAAGTE

The advance into Natal was being carried out by four distinct forces. Erasmus and Meyer had converged on Dundee while away to the south west Prinsloo's Orange Free State forces were moving east towards Ladysmith. Between Dundee and Ladysmith stood the Biggarsberg hills and the little coal-mining village of Elandslaagte, through which the railway passed and where the roads from Newcastle and from Glencoe and Dundee met. From Botha's Pass in the Drackensberg mountains the Johannesburgers under General Kock rode to occupy these hills. While the British were attacking the Boers on Talana Hill, Kock's commando was attempting to capture trains. One escaped, but a second drew into Elandslaagte station and was taken, together with its consignment of whisky. The rest of the Boer force arrived that evening and the next day the train was unloaded and some attention was given to establishing defences round the town. That evening the booty was consumed and captors and captives together sang and drank at the hotel. In the meanwhile Major-general Sir John French had been carrying out reconnaissance and on

Right **The Battle of Elandslaagte, according to Maurice's** *History of the War in South Africa*. **The road layout today is a little different, but the remains of the coal workings north of the station can still be seen.** (McM. MFME BW10/12)

Below **The Boer Memorial crowns the little hill at the northern end of their position and beyond lies the plain over which they were pursued by the Lancers.** (MFME BW9/9)

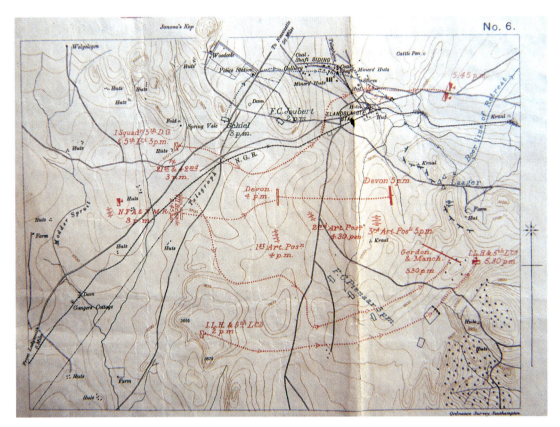

Left **The memorials to Colonel Scott Chisholme, 5th Lancers, and the Imperial Light Horse which he commanded at Elandslaagte.** (MFME BW9/6)

Below **A plaque lists the 26 burghers who fell at Elandslaagte and were later reinterred on the Platrand, Ladysmith.** (MFME BW9/10)

Bottom **The Gordon Highlanders memorial stands in the little graveyard below the slope up which they advanced.** (MFME BW8/27)

the morning of 21 October he arrived with five squadrons of the Imperial Light Horse and the Natal Field Battery. The captured railway staff and the Boers had a rude awakening after their night of partying.

The Boers opened fire from the gun emplacements they had established on the hills a little over a mile to the south-east of the station and French telegraphed for reinforcements. They were substantial. Colonel Ian Hamilton arrived at about three o'clock in the afternoon in command of the infantry, seven companies of the 1st Devonshire Regiment, five of the 2nd Gordon Highlanders and the 1st Manchester Regiment. They detrained about two miles short of the station, where now a little graveyard stands by the track. There were also a squadron each of the 5th Lancers and the 5th Dragoon Guards and two batteries of Field Artillery, giving French a total force of some 3,500 men. The Devons were to advance on the left, the Manchesters in the centre and the Gordons on the right to take the Boers in the flank. There was little cover, the country being open but strewn with rocks. The Devons moved forward in open formation to engage the bulk of the Boer force with the artillery providing covering fire, then the Manchesters and Gordons moved forward, but were pinned down by the counter-fire from rifles and artillery. The skies grew dark as a rainstorm swept over the field and both Hamilton and French urged the men to greater efforts. The Gordons got entangled in a wire fence which had to be uprooted post by post before they could pass. General Kock himself led a counter-attack and fell in the act. The Imperial Light Horse, now dismounted, as eager to avenge Majuba as were the Gordons, rushed forward and the Boers

broke and fled. Trooper E. H. Cross of the Imperial Light Horse wrote to his father in New South Wales:

'I send you papers with a fair account of our Battle of Elandslaagte. We had a awful time of it, and I saw sights I shall never forget. I am sorry our Colonel Chisholme was shot. He was leading us right through the thick of it, and as proud of his youngsters as possible.'

A Prussian, Colonel Schiel, was wounded in the legs and taken prisoner. He wrote to a friend in North Sydney:

'It was a strange feeling at Elandslaagte, when lying wounded on the battlefield and recovering from unconsciousness. The first faces I saw were Johannesburg friends in the Imperial Light Horse. The officer who took me prisoner was one of my best friends, an Australian named Karri Davies. That really is the fortune of war.'

As the Boers rode north-east in the gathering dusk the Lancers and the Dragoons swept across their line of retreat, cutting down fleeing men and, no doubt, in the fury of the charge, some attempting to surrender as well. They reformed and charged back, inflicting further loss on men who did not comprehend this way of war. It had been a text-book European action – artillery fire followed by infantry attack culminating in cavalry charge. The Boers thought white men should not fight with spears. J. G. Dunn, an American serving with the Irish Brigade alongside the Boers, wrote revealingly,

'The Lancers acted as if fighting Indians, and gave no quarter, stabbing and murdering … That lot of gentry are down in our black book … if the opportunity presents itself … we will wipe them off the rolls.'

It is not clear whether he meant the Lancers fought as if they were Indians or as if the Boers were.

YULE'S RETREAT

While the British were thoroughly pleased with themselves, their position was not good. At Dundee they were almost surrounded and under fire from the Creusot, at Elandslaagte they had thrown the Johannesburgers back but at Ladysmith they faced the influx of Prinsloo's men from the west. General White was obliged to order the evacuation of Dundee. He could not reinforce the town and Yule could not be expected to hold it. The Boers dominated the route to Glencoe from the height of Impati, leaving only one way out, the eastern road running south towards Helpmekaar and Rorke's Drift from which Yule could cut across south of Elandslaagte, with luck being able to ford the three rivers between Dundee and Ladysmith, and provided the Boers did not realise what was going on.

Major Wickham of the Indian Commissariat managed to sneak back into the abandoned camp and get 33 wagons out with various supplies for the three-day march they faced. By 9pm he was ready to move off. Candles were lit in abandoned tents and the hospital camp with the wounded of Talana, including Penn Symons, was left in the care of Major J. F. Donegan, the chief medical officer. Messages were still being telegraphed out at 11.30pm after the 4,500 men, brilliantly marshalled and controlled in the darkness, were on the march for Ladysmith. By dawn on Monday 23 October they were able to pause for breakfast and enjoy the rising sun.

The Boers' inability to pursue is a mystery. They were shelling Dundee again that Monday morning and as noon approached Donegan sent a man under flag of truce to ask for a ceasefire. The Boers entered the town, as Reitz recalls:

'... *We were anxious to be first in ... By now Maroola's men were also making for Dundee, galloping hard behind us, but we were well in advance and easily got in before they came. They were not long, however, and soon 1,500 men were whooping through the streets, and behaving in a very undisciplined manner ... we plundered shops and dwelling-houses ... It was not for what we could get out of it, for we knew that we could carry little or nothing away with us, but the joy of ransacking other people's property is hard to resist ...*'

As darkness fell a token force from Meyer's commando went looking for Yule's column, but it was already on the move once more, pushing on to van Tonders pass. It was not until 10am the next day that the whole force reached the Waschbank river, having struggled in the dark over rough and broken roads. The morning passed in a reconnoitre to the west, where gunfire was heard, but Yule returned to the main body in the afternoon and started to cross the river. A sudden storm swelled the steam to a torrent, and some men had to remain on the northern side until the next day. The gunfire they had heard was the action at Reitfontein, in which White prevented the Free Staters from cutting off Yule's approach to safety. Among the Boers there was Christiaan De Wet, in temporary command of the Heilbron commando. He later believed that he had missed Yule through Boer delays in advance, but in this he was mistaken, and it must be remembered that his account was written on board ship, en route to Europe, after the war and without access to notes, diaries or the works of others. He says:

'We had to be prepared for an attack from their combined forces [in this he is mistaken; Yule had not yet arrived], and that before the Transvaalers, who were still at Dundee, could reinforce us. The British did not keep us long in anxiety.

'At eight o'clock … the 24th of October … the battle of Modder Spruit [or Reitfontein] began… We occupied kopjes which formed a large semicircle to the west of the railway between Ladysmith and Dundee. Our only gun was placed on the side of a high kop on our western wing…

'With three batteries of guns the English marched to the attack, the troops leading the way, the guns some distance behind. A deafening carronade was opened on us by the enemy's artillery, at a range of about 4,500 yards [4.1km]. Our gun fired a few shots in return, but was soon silenced …'

The British pressured the Boers until 3pm, moving forward under cover, but unable to get close enough to charge. Heavy rifle fire was exchanged, but no advantage was gained by either side and, in the mid-afternoon, the British withdrew. De Wet congratulated his men on their stand, but it was probably a holding action by both sides.

At 4am on Wednesday, 25 October, Yule's column was on the move again, crossing the Sunday's River by noon and stopping to rest and eat. That afternoon

they made contact with a patrol of the Border Mounted Rifles from Ladysmith and learnt that a relief column under Lieutenant-colonel J. A. Coxhead was to guide them in. But now the worst of the journey tormented them. Darkness fell early as the rain lashed down again – the road became a mud wallow. Wagons were abandoned, soldiers fell asleep into the mire, and still the staggering men struggled on. A mile to the east of the pass between Mbulwana and Lombards Kop Coxhead waited. At 4.30am on 26 October the first of Yule's men arrived and it was noon before all were into Ladysmith. It took three days for the men to recover from their ordeal, and some never did. Brigadier-general Yule was invalided home, having saved one third of White's army, not by dramatic heroics, but by cool, calculated and ruthless efficiency that commanded little admiration at the time.

NICHOLSON'S NEK

With the Boers gathering about Ladysmith General White devised a scheme to roll up their line before it was fully formed. Deneys Reitz was in the Boer advance.

'Next day our whole line moved forward, and a fine sight it was, as the masses of horsemen breasted the green slopes towards the final hills from which we could look down to Ladysmith… By night our men had occupied Bulwana and Lombaardskop, two prominent heights [to the east of Ladysmith], and they were also holding a line

Left **Hairy Mary, the engine of the armoured train reinforced with rope-work protection. This marvel was created with 2,000 fathoms of 6in. rope by men of HMS *Terrible* at Chieveley.** (McM. MFME BW12/7)

*that stretched around [the north] by Pepworth's Hill and
the ridges lying towards Nicholson's Nek [to the west]… A
collision with the British was imminent.'*

Reitz does not mention Long Hill which lies east
of Pepworth on the other side of the road northwards
to Newcastle and which was to be the principal
objective of the action of 30 October. Colonel G. G.
Grimwood was to lead the 8th Brigade against Meyer's
commando on that hill, supported by 7th Brigade
under Ian Hamilton moving towards Pepworth which
they were to take once Grimwood had secured Long
Hill. General French's cavalry would protect the right

flank and Lieutenant-colonel F. R. C. Carleton was to
take a force of infantry and a mountain battery to hold
the pass called Nicholson's Nek, north of Ladysmith,
through which the defeated Boers were expected to
flee.

In addition to the complexity this plan already
presented in terms of command and control, all troops
were to move into position by night. Carleton moved
off from the rendezvous close to the junction of the
Newcastle and Harrismith railway lines at 11.15pm on
Sunday, 29 October with six companies of 1st The
Royal Irish Fusiliers, 10th Mountain Battery and five
and a half companies (450 men) of 1st The
Gloucestershire Regiment. There were 137 men of the
Mountain Battery with six guns, dismantled for
carriage, and 600 rounds of ammunition on 133
mules attended by 52 Cape 'Boys'. The total force
comprised 1,149 men and 250 animals, of which 100
or so were carrying supplies and ammunition for the
infantry. They made their way north alongside Bell
Spruit, into the flat-bottomed valley between the slope
that rose to Pepworth on their right and the hill of
Tchrengula which ran north in a series of summits to
Nicholson's Nek. Progress was slow, the road being
rough and men stumbling and blundering about in
the night. By 1am they had got no further than level
with the southern spur of Tchrengula, about two miles
short of their objective.

Carleton became apprehensive. The possibility of
being caught in this narrowing valley as dawn broke
seemed very great. He decided to climb to the top of
Tchrengula and establish a position of defence. The
ascent was perilous and soon men and mules were

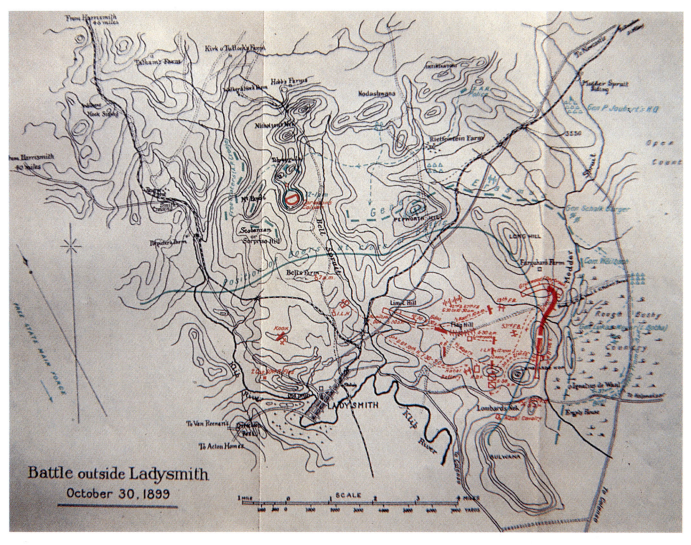

Battle outside Ladysmith
October 30, 1899

tripping and slipping in the dark until first one, then another mule panicked and soon there was a general stampede down the slope, men and animals bellowing and falling. The guns were gone, as was the infantry's ammunition reserve. The men gathered themselves and the remnants of the mule train together and clambered on to the top. As dawn broke they were busy building sangars of the rocks strewn about the hilltop. From the east Deneys Reitz and his companions opened fire across the valley and a piquet on Surprise Hill did the same. Commandant van Dam brought 400 ZARPs to Nicholson's Nek where he found Commandant Steenkamp and Christiaan De Wet with some 150 Free Staters. They moved along the heights towards the British finding them, according to De Wet, well placed in cover to the south of fairly open space.

'At the northern end, where we were, the surface was smooth, but somewhat further south it became rough and stony, affording very good cover… There were a number of ruined Kaffir kraals scattered about from the middle of the mountain to its southern end, and these the enemy

had occupied, thus securing a great advantage. Our bullets hailed on the English, and very shortly they retreated to the southernmost part of the mountain. This gave us the chance for which we had been waiting, for now we could take the splendid positions they had left.'

Confusion over signals amongst the British had led to the retreat. The line stretched over the top of the hill, the Gloucesters on the left and the Irish on the right and communication between the units was faulty. Early in the afternoon white flags appeared somewhere on the left while the Irish fought on. In even greater muddle Carleton felt he could not disavow the white flag, for the Boers were rising from their positions, accepting the surrender. Officers had to wrestle rifles from their men, anger, tears and disbelief greeted the order to submit. An officer later declared, 'We were surrendered against our will'. Thirty-seven officers and 917 men were taken prisoner while 69 lay dead and 249 were wounded.

Against Long Hill and Pepworth the failure was more modest. At daylight Grimwood found himself without half his force and facing the wrong place, for

Above **Ladysmith, the operations of 30 October as mapped in** *The Times History of the War in South Africa*. **Nicholson's Nek is north of the town.** (TM. MFME BW3/14)

Right **The graves of men of the Irish Fusiliers, the Mountain Battery and the Gloucesters on the top of Tchrengula.** (McM. MFME BW10/32)

Below **A 155mm Creusot 'Long Tom' being moved to Ladysmith.** (McM. MFME BW10/36)

there were no longer Boers on Long Hill. Nor was French's cavalry to be seen. Beyond the Modder River, newly in command of what had been the now invalid Lucas Meyer's commando, Louis Botha lay in wait with some 4,000 men. The enfilading fire staggered Grimwood's men. Hamilton's troops had to be diverted from Pepworth Hill, now crowned with a Boer 'Long Tom', to support the hard-pressed 8th Brigade before all were withdrawn, around noon, to Ladysmith. Deneys Reitz was by then on top of Tchrengula amidst the surrendering Irish Fusiliers.

'Shortly after the surrender I was talking to some of the captured officers when I heard one of them exclaim, "My God; look there!" and turning round we saw the entire British force that had come out against us on the plain that morning in full retreat to Ladysmith. Great clouds of dust billowed over the Veldt as the troops withdrew, and the manner of their going had every appearance of a rout... To our surprise there was no pursuit. I heard Christiaan De Wet mutter, "Los jou ruiters; los jou ruiters" (loose your horsemen - loose your horsemen), but the Commandant-General let this wonderful opportunity go by... I was told by old Maroola [Erasmus] himself, that when officers came up to implore Piet Joubert to follow, he quoted the Dutch

saying, *"When God holds out a finger, don't take the whole hand."'*

Only the artillery, the 13th, 53rd and 21st Batteries, gained any distinction, and that for the covering of a retreat. It was Mournful Monday indeed.

THE INVESTMENT OF LADYSMITH

As Sir Redvers Buller was arriving in Cape Town on the Tuesday, the net was closing on Ladysmith and the heavy Creusot, the Long Tom on Pepworth, had started its work. General White was already aware of the Boer superiority in heavy artillery, and on 25 October had telegraphed Rear Admiral Sir Robert Harris at Simonstown, 'The Boer guns are greatly outranging my guns. Can you let me have a few Naval guns?' Harris passed the problem to Captain Percy Scott of HMS *Terrible*, together with *Powerful* one of two cruisers 1st class, in Simon Bay. Scott had already designed a field gun carriage for the ship's 12-pdrs. and had four of them contructed. He remarked:

'I had great difficulty in convincing the authorities that it was not a toy ... the mounting looked rather amateurish.'

Where everyone else pronounced the impossibility of such a thing, Scott had no hesitation in saying he could have plans ready for mounting a 4.7in. gun for land use by the following day. He decided on a timber mounting in the shape of a cross, the four great baulks to be transported broken down and bolted together where needed. At 5pm the next day HMS *Powerful* sailed for Durban with the three 12-pdrs. and two 4.7ins., complete with mountings. In the forenoon of Mournful Monday the guns reached Ladysmith. Bella Craw, 33 years old, stayed in Ladysmith with her mother and sister and wrote on Monday, 30 October:

'What an awful day we have had, we none of us shall ever forget it... At precisely ten minutes past five we heard the first shell. We laid still for five minutes, then they went on hot and strong. We got dressed, then strolled up the

street… While we were talking and the boom of cannon going every few seconds, another shell from "Big Tom" as we call it, burst not far away… Aunt Fanny, Uncle William, Norman and I walked up the hill behind the Convent to see what we could of the battle. With powerful field glasses we could see the shells falling all round "Long Tom", but the Boers always kept under cover… Just before lunch we heard the shout of "Baas Buyela!" We all ran down and had only just got on the back veranda when the whirr of a shell sounded in the air and a piece of the shell fell a few feet from us. This was the last from "Long Tom", as three large Marine guns arrived just in the nick of time. They arrived at the station and were taken to position without any loss of time, and after three shots "Long Tom" was silenced, they say for only twenty-four hours though.'

The 4.7in. guns had a range of some 10,000 yards (5.7mi/9km) against the 11,000 yards (6.25mi/10km) of the Creusots and the 12-pdrs. 8,000 yards (4.5mi/7.3km) as against the 8,500 yards (4.8mi/7.8km) of the Boer 75mm guns. Something close to parity, given that the army's 12-pdr. had a range of only 5,200 yards (3mi/4.8km) firing high explosive and a mere 3,800 yards (2.2mi/3.5km) with shrapnel. Captain Scott had proposed that 5,000 rounds should be sent with the 4.7ins. Admiral Harris authorised 500 which, as Scott remarked, would last 25 minutes at 10 rounds per minute, but it may be doubted that larger supplies would have arrived in time to beat the Boer embrace of the town. The Naval Brigade also brought four Vickers-Maxims and the ammunition actually with them was: for 4.7ins, 200 rounds each of common shell, Lyddite and shrapnel; for 12-pdrs., 738 common shell, 396 shrapnel and 24 case shot; Lee-Metford ammunition, besides the 150 rounds carried by each man, 39,000 rounds; for Maxims 64,000 rounds and for revolvers 5,400 rounds.

While many people were leaving Ladysmith for the south, others were arriving. Kate Driver, at twenty-four years of age, had been a qualified nurse for two years when, on 22 October, she left Pietermaritzburg for Ladysmith on the 9am train. She arrived in the controlled chaos of the aftermath of the battle at Enlandslaagte and was immediately thrown into the buzz of activity settling patients in the marquees erected alongside the Town Hall and the Public Library. It was midnight before she could seek her billet. She wrote to her mother:

'And oh I would be glad if you would send me a couple of brown holland dresses. My tussore silk ones get fearfully long in the rain and the mud gets on to them

Left **A map of operations in northern Natal from** *The Times History*, **which gives a fair impression of the events before the siege of Ladysmith and its attempted relief introduced static warfare.** (TM. MFME BW3/16)

Above right **The site of the ambush of the armoured train and Churchill's capture (p. 32). Looking back to Estcourt, a modern train emerges from the railway cutting and a vehicle approaches on the Estcourt road. In the curve of the track below the truck the graveyard can be seen. To the right, between the tree and the minibus, the white stone of the memorial is visible.** (MFME BW16/28)

Below right **Looking towards Colenso, the original rail embankment can be seen, together with an intermediate and final raising of the track-bed to its current height. The Boer guns were on the hill to the left. The modern road to Chieveley runs to the left of the old road which crossed the river close to the old embankment.** (MFME BW16/34)

about a foot deep. You can imagine what I look like! Today they have been fixing a balloon. I suppose it will be sent up tomorrow to find the Boers.'

Bella Craw saw the balloon as well.

'… *We went to see the Observation Balloon. It ascends 900ft. and if penetrated by a bullet it makes no*

difference but closes up again. The men working it telephone the position of the enemy.'

On Thursday 2 November Major George Tatham, Bella's uncle, who was in command of the Lady-smith troop of the Natal Carbineers, noted in his diary:

'Rail stopped… Many women and children left… We laid in a stock of provisions etc. for a few weeks. This order of wife's I told Messrs Sparks Bros. to duplicate, feeling sure we should be shut in for a month or two. Went out with about 500 volunteers, a small lot of Lancers and a battery of Artillery round End Hill. At 4pm saw Boer Commando from O.F.S. out-spanned [unharnessed] near Table Hill [Grobler's Kop]. Fired a few shots at them and we ordered to retire. General French was in charge and left Ladysmith that night by last train.'

The town was besieged. There were 5,500 white civilians, 2,500 Africans and Indians and 13,500 officers and men in Ladysmith.

THE THRUST FOR DURBAN
Durban was alive with activity. Captain Percy Scott was appointed Military Governor and Commandant of Durban on 3 November and the *Terrible* immediately left for Natal. The Naval defence force landed there on 8 November and Scott made his dispositions for the defence of the town and the perimeter was secured before evening. Martial law was declared and suspected spies rounded up. Defences were also built at Pietermaritzburg and throughout the colony a frenzy of recruiting raised the Imperial Infantry Corps, Murray's Mounted Volunteers, Thorneycroft's Mounted Infantry, the Umvoti Mounted Volunteers and the Durban Light Infantry.

The initial advance by the Boers south of Ladysmith was under the command of Louis Botha. He made his way through the hills north of the Tugela River and over it into Colenso. The people and farmers quit the area as he approached. Mr Clouston wrote to his son who was on the family farm of that

name to instruct him to put his wife and children on the train, to bury the guns, sporting rifles, in a given place and to drive the cattle south. The sheep he would have to abandon. The young man dutifully did as he was told, pausing only to change into his better clothes before departing. Some weeks later a letter from Botha reached him. It thanked him for leaving a note in the pocket of his working jacket letting them know where the guns were, and mentioned that the mutton was delicious.

The advance towards Pietermaritzburg and Durban was tentative. On 3 November the Boers went on from Colenso the five miles to Chieveley but failed to reach Estcourt before the arrival of Major-general H. J. T. Hildyard with the first of his brigade and

elements of volunteer units. A Queenslander, Trooper T. Sulivan, was serving with the Natal Mounted Police, and was out scouting when he and his companion were cut off by a large body of Boers. Riding cross-country to regain their camp, they came up with a group of five Boers and engaged them, killing two, wounding a third and capturing two more.

'I tied their horses together, my comrade taking the leading rein. I followed up the rear with a stick, and we were on our way … But when our plan was seen by the main body of Boers we were hotly pursued for a distance of 8 miles.'

They made it back to Escourt and Hildyard was so pleased that he took Sulivan onto his personal bodyguard.

Meanwhile the decision to seriously invade the territory south of the Tugela was just being taken. Joubert was in debate with his commandants and the Free Staters. These last refused to go forward, but on 13 November Joubert and Botha led 1,500 Transvaalers and 500 Free Staters of independent mind down to the Tugela to cross the next day. The British had maintained a clumsy contact with the front, using an armoured train. It had entered Colenso on 5 November and recovered four wagon loads of provisions and ammunition, but four days later found the line torn up south of the village. In spite of the evident presence of the enemy, the armoured train continued to undertake its journeys, unsupported by other troops and a tempting target for a mobile force.

On 15 November the train chuffed off again, carrying men to repair the track and manned by 120 men of the Dublin Fusiliers and the Durban Light Infantry under Captain J. A. L. Haldane, together with some naval ratings with a muzzle-loading 7-pdr. gun from HMS *Tartar*. Along for the ride was a newspaper correspondent, with military experience in the Sudan, by the name of Winston Churchill.

A few Boers were seen in the distance as the train ran up to Chieveley, pushing an ordinary wagon with the 7-pdr. in it and an armoured wagon with loopholes and an open top in front of the engine and tender, and pulling two more armoured cars and an open wagon with repair materials in it behind. Beyond Chieveley the Boers were to be seen in numbers, so the telegraphist reported to Colonel C. J. Long in Estcourt and got the message to withdraw. So back they went, the truck of materials first. Some four miles (6km) south the land rises and then drops away gently to the crossing of the Bloukrans River before entering a cutting. Since then the railtrack has been raised, probably twice, but the original route can be seen, turning sharply left after coming over the river, and here a guard rail was once fixed to prevent complete disaster if the train took the curve too fast. Here the Boers had placed stones.

As the train approached the ridge Botha opened fire with two 75mm guns and a pom-pom. The driver accelerated to get away, careered down the slope and hit the stones. The materials wagon was thrown in the air and fell on the embankment, the next carried on for a bit and then fell on its side, spilling out its troops. The third wagon was derailed but stayed upright and the rest of the train halted, but still on the rails. The Boers moved swiftly to resume fire. Churchill was in the armoured wagon that was now behind the engine and popped out to see what was going on. He came back to tell Haldane the line could be cleared and the Fusiliers kept up their fire. The 7-pdr. had not long been in action before being silenced. Boer shells passed clean through the armour without exploding. Shells found on the field of action since have still had their safety fuses in place; in the heat of battle the Boers had neglected to arm them. As the shells and bullets fizzed past, Churchill and the Durban Light Infantry struggled to push the half-derailed truck fully off the line, and then to move it yet further to allow the

engine to pass. No sooner had they succeeded than the trucks to the rear of the engine became detatched, so the wounded were piled on the tender, clung to the engine or crammed into the cab with the wounded driver, while the fit ran alongside. As the engine increased its speed and drew away someone amongst those left behind on foot waved a handkerchief and the Boers rode forward to take the surrender. Churchill himself was caught in the railway cutting.

As he was taken towards captivity in Pretoria, two statements were made to Churchill both of which were typical of Boer attitudes. One young man said, 'If I thought that the Dutchmen would give in because Pretoria was taken, I would smash my rifle ...

Above **The Scottish Rifles march into Estcourt.** (McM. MFME BW11/5)

Above right **The grave of men of the Durban Light Infantry, the lettering marked out with .303 cartridge cases.** (MFME BW16/32)

Right **Three generations of Boers; a classic photograph, inscribed with the names and ages of the men.** (McM. MFME BW11/24)

Left **Shell damage to the derailed armoured train.** (McM. MFME BW10/26)

this very moment. We will fight for ever.' At Volkrust he was introduced to the man who had blocked the track and caused the derailment, and who had been rewarded with 14 days' leave to go home and see his wife. 'Surely,' Churchill said, 'this is a very critical time to leave the front. You may miss an important battle.' 'Yes,' came the honest reply, 'I hope so.'

Joubert and Botha continued their foray into southern Natal by bypassing Estcourt in two groups, east and west, and meeting to cut the railway line at Willow Grange on 21 November. Scouting parties went even further south, Free Staters to Mooirivier and to Nottingham Road, but no further. At 2pm on 22 November the Natal Carbineers escorted a force from Estcourt to Willow Grange and, that night, helped heave a naval 12-pdr. to the north-east shoulder of Beacon Hill in torrrential rain, through mud and over rocks that capsized the weapon. Once righted they pushed on, but came under fire from the Boers before managing to get their gun emplaced. In the dark the West Yorkshires and East Surreys advanced on Harris Hill on which the Boers had established themselves and in the storm they went up on both sides of a wall. Mistaking each other for the enemy, they opened fire for a moment, but nonetheless took the ridge. As day broke they came under Boer fire from positions the naval gun could not locate and so they withdrew. By noon they were back in Estcourt.

The Boers, too, had had enough. Botha was eager to push on, but Joubert was exhausted. Before the conference could convene to discuss the matter Joubert was thrown from his horse and injured. That was the last straw, and back they went, north of the Tugela. Joubert returned home, a sick and broken man, leaving Louis Botha in command. The offensive was over. Botha turned his attention to the siege of Ladysmith and the conversion of the Tugela line into a formidable system of defence against Buller's forthcoming attack. Christiaan De Wet was to observe,

' ... *Whatever his own people have to say to his discredit, Sir Redvers Buller had to operate against stronger positions than any other English General in South Africa.*'

THE BRITISH OFFENSIVE

On 30 October Sir Redvers Buller arrived in Cape Town and within three days had been reduced to a mood of deep pessimism. Sir Alfred Milner was downcast at the reverses already experienced and within a week the siege of Ladysmith was an established fact. Buller wrote to his brother:

'I am in the tightest place I have ever been in, and the worst of it is I think nothing of my own creating – I don't know if I can get out of it alright, and I think if I fail it is fair my family should know afterwards what at any rate I had to say on my own defence.'

In addition to events in Natal, at Mafeking and at Kimberley, there was the possibility of a rising by the Dutch in Cape Colony; indeed, it was confidently expected to take place any minute by the Boers themselves. Buller pulled the garrisons out of Naauwpoort and Stormberg lest they, too, were besieged.

It appeared that Durban was under a real threat and also that Kimberley was in danger of being surrendered. Cecil Rhodes had contrived to get himself shut up in the town and Milner was bombarded with messages, culminating on this of 31 October:

'... Now that the General has arrived we respectfully request to be informed as to the policy to be adopted regarding relief, so as to enable us to take our own steps in case relief refused.'

Coming from the Directors of De Beers, this was a clear threat to surrender Kimberley if they were not satisfied with Buller's plans. The garrison was commanded by Lieutenant-colonel Kekewich who was hampered by a progressively worsening relationship with Rhodes, in spite of which he was to conduct the defence with distinction. It was impossible to choose between the two theatres of war; the British forces would have to be divided.

On the western flank, along the railway to Kimberley, Lieutenant-general Lord Methuen was given the task of relieving that town with the 1st Division. In the centre, on the rail lines up from Port Elizabeth via Nauuwpoort and from East London via Stormberg, Lieutenant-general Sir William Gatacre's 3rd Division, less Major-general Hart's brigade which had been sent to Natal, would secure the Cape border against Boer incursions. In Natal Buller would himself

take command, thus achieving proximity to one front rather than none. On 22 November he left Cape Town in secret.

THE DRIVE FOR KIMBERLEY

Lieutenant Barton and the 2nd Northamptons (previously the 58th) arrived in Cape Town on 13 November, but could not disembark until the next day because of rough seas. At 8am they docked and found the railway alongside the ship, requiring baggage and stores to be moved only a few yards. They had little time to appreciate the joys of the town or admire the view. Half the Scots Guards left at 11am, the rest of them at 4.40pm and at 5pm the 58th were on their way,

'... amidst a good deal of cheering from town loafers in the streets through which the line to the quay runs ... The carriages are good but the men closely packed 6 or 8 per compartment which is rather close for a journey of 36 hours to De Aar Junction if we do not go on the extra 70 to Orange River Bridge...

'As we left the sunset upon Table Mountain was glorious. We had what some would call a makeshift meal

Left **A British supply convoy, drawn by oxen and mules, crosses a drift.** (McM. MFME BW16/3)

Above right **A map of the action at Belmont from *The Times History*.** (TM. MFME BW3/17)

Right **Belmont station is among the trees in the middle distance and the Boer monument crowns Gun Hill. Beyond the monument is the country over which the British made their advance.** (MFME BW12/34)

in the train at 7.20, but to me it was a most enjoyable picnic; cold salt beef eaten with a knife on a slice of bread, potted meat on biscuits, chocolate, and fresh strawberries, this hardly sounds like soldiering on active service it all seems one grand tourist trip …'

Barton did admit that the officers were comfortably placed and wished more could be done for the men. Breakfast was taken at Matjesfontein at 9.30am. For the men, tea, bully beef and biscuit. To Barton's embarrassment, the officers were served chops, ham and eggs. The time would come, he thought, when the officers would have to show that they could share the same conditions as the men.

On reaching De Aar on 16 November they were ordered to push on immediately after drawing their transport, which Barton described as:

'7 Buck Wagons with teams of 10 mules each also mules for machine gun team of 5 looks like Horse Artillery rather.'

To their delight the right half of the battalion arrived the next day,

'… so now the 58th Regiment is complete & ready for the "return match" it has longed for since Laings Nek. [Where the British were defeated in the First Boer War.] Nothing could be more fortunate than what has happened to us, arranged for by the War Office …'

The Northamptons were brigaded with the Yorkshire Light Infantry, who were three months in the country from India, the 5th (Northumberland) Fusiliers, and a half battalion of the Loyal North Lancashire Regiment, the other half being in Kimberley. The rest of the force was made up of the Guards Brigade, two batteries of field artillery and four Navy 12-pdrs., four companies of Engineers and too few horsemen. There was one Regular cavalry regiment, the 9th Lancers to which was attached the squadron of the New South Wales Lancers that had come out from England. In addition there were Rimington's Guides, 200 locally raised troops under Major M. F. Rimington and about 100 Mounted Infantry. As Barton observed, that made up the Division

'… under that well known General, Methuen & from what we can see he is preparing to strike hard & rapidly. One step he has taken as an example of his practical methods: officers are to discard their useless swords & carry rifles or carbines so as to confuse the Boer marksmen. All the old Aldershot Drill Book Tactics are to be abolished & we shall adopt very extended order, men getting quickly from rock to rock, irregularity of line being sought & "regular dressing" being avoided.

'18th Nov. Sat. Battalion practised attack formations in consort with Yorkshire Light Infantry.

'21st Nov. Tuesday. Whole division left Orange River at dawn as a lightly equipped expedition men having only a blanket apiece & a waterproof sheet between two besides what they stood up in and the greatcoat they carried …'

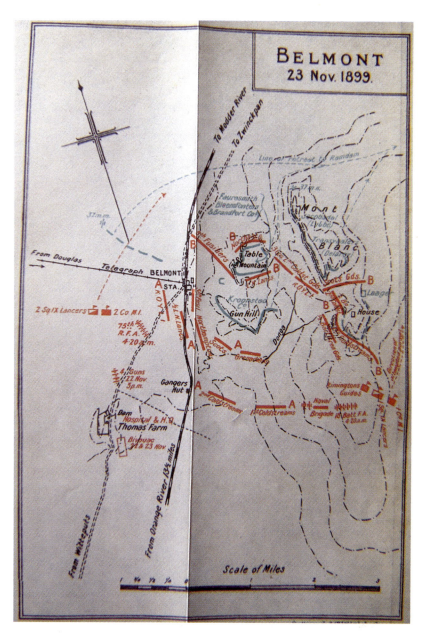

Above **Near the bivouac area close to Thomas's Farm stands the Guards Memorial.** (MFME BW13/3)

Below **A photograph of the terrain at Belmont from Barton's journal.** (NRA. MFME BW17/27)

The rest of their stores were to follow by rail or in the mule wagons. Methuen expected his first encounter with the Boers to be at Belmont, a hamlet and railway station some 15 miles (24km) north of Orange River where a line of kopjes ran north to south, overlooking the railway and road from the east. The Division marched along by the railway line over flat, dry country, overlooked here and there by abrupt hills rising from the plain like children's sandcastles. Scouting undetected in such country was not possible. They halted at Witput Station where Barton reports a fine reservoir of beautiful water, a welcome change from the 'rather thick' water at Orange River.

BELMONT

That afternoon the scouts were fired on by the Boers from kopjes overlooking the railway and road six miles further on, near Belmont. At 4pm on Wednesday 22 November the main body moved off towards Belmont, cavalry and artillery preceding the 58th which formed the infantry advance guard. A few shots failed to inconvenience them as they moved, Barton says, into Belmont, actually Thomas's Farm about two miles west of the rail station, where the guns unlimbered and shelled the hills some three miles (5km) beyond. There they slept until 2.30am when they moved off once more, the 9th Brigade to attack the kopje to the north, Table Mountain, and the Guards Brigade to take Gun Hill, the two miles of open country to be traversed in the dark and the attack to go in at dawn. The cavalry were to outflank the position to the south.

They moved off on time. Barton reports:

'The first shots were fired soon after 4am. The bullets now began to whistle & scream while the outline of the hills was lit up with brilliant flashes as we got near the foot of them. The hail rendered it advisable to get flat on the stomach & so complete the remaining 100 yards [90m] to the mountain. A spur ... [under Gun Hill] affording cover from the fire of Table Mountain, a lot of us made for it & found the Scots Guards lying in a huge mass there waiting for the other Guards to secure their points of attack further to the right. Their pipers played The Cock of the North & other airs but as they were lying flat on their backs the music was also rather flat.'

Colonel Denny pushed his men forward and Lieutenant Skinner led a group along beneath the hill to their left, whence they made their way up to the col and there opened fire on the flank of the Boer position to their north. They could see only a couple of men, but the fire was heavy enough to convince them they needed reinforcements. More men climbed up to them, Guards, Fusiliers and 58th, and joined in firing on the Boer positions.

'We could not see the men amongst the boulders so as to get a fair shot at them, to advance directly on them we had to climb over the boulders & they picked off any man who showed himself.'

Then the Guards, who had taken Gun Hill, came across the upland on the Northampton's right. The 58th also turned north and moved against the Boer position.

'Worming my way among the boulders here I felt a sharp smack on the head which made a singing in my

ears, but absolutely no pain. It did not take long to whip out the field dressing & a pad of antiseptic wool soon began to staunch the blood. The Boers were now being surrounded & hoisted a shirt but it was some little time before the firing stopped on both sides. Knight the War Correspondent of the Morning Post was hit after they had the flag of truce up.'

Barton bound up the newspaperman's wound, and seems to have taken the neglect of the white flag as amateurish incompetence. The battle had lasted three and a half hours and ended, unknown to Barton, as the Boers withdrew, mounted, and rode away. The cavalry were too fatigued to give chase. He commented,

'The Grenadiers seem to have had some very hard fighting & had a terrible loss. A number of the 58th were with them but we had drummed it into the men that they must keep widely extended so that they kept about 6 or 10 paces apart while the Grenadiers were crowded to 1 pace apart & suffered accordingly. Their fearless advance must have astonished the Boers very much.'

Major V. C. M. Sellheim, a Queenslander, was serving with the Northamptons as a Special Service Officer. He wrote home:

'I was in the thick of it all day with the Northamptons … Our casualties were 231. I saw some ghastly sights, and felt at the time that war was a very horrible business. The hottest corner I was in was a valley between two kopjes. It rained a hail of lead there, and we had to take what shelter we could get, while the artillery fired over our heads and shelled the Boers out… Our infantry are wonderful, and had a very difficult task to storm these kopjes covered with boulders.'

The artillery fire Sellheim speaks of was probably laid down by the Naval 12-pdrs. of HMS Doris under Captain R. C. Prothero who said:

'I … had great difficulty in taking my heavy ammunition wagons and guns across the railway line, finally succeeding… I then turned to the left between two kopjes, and found the Boers on the rear kopje, firing upon advancing infantry. I immediately got the battery into action, and at 1,700 yards [1.6km] shelled the Boers, *who were firing on our troops, the practice being excellent. The Boers were very soon silenced and retreated.'*

An attempt to reposition the guns on a kopje to harass the retreating Boers had to be abandoned because of the roughness of the terrain, 'it was impossible to take wheels over it', Prothero remarked. With two trains in attendance the advance towards Kimberley resumed early in the afternoon.

GRASPAN

Lieutenant Barton was not with the Northamptons as they moved on. To his anger and disgust, what he claimed was a superficial and trivial knock on the head was seen by the Medical Officer as a wound requiring hospital treatment; indeed, other medics agreed and Barton was sent back to Cape Town.

That evening the Naval Brigade, some 400 men strong, were told they would have a part to play in attacking an equal number of Boers just seen on the kopjes between Graspan and Enslin, said to be commanded by De la Rey. They were delighted, except for those who had to stay with the guns. They had arrived too late to be more than witnesses to the fight at Belmont, other than their four 12-pdrs. At 3am on Saturday, 25 November, 245 sailors stood to arms and moved to the assembly point. Unknown to the British, Prinsloo had arrived to bring the Boer strength up to some 2,000 men.

The kopjes stand in a rough line running east from the railway which kinks around the western end and as the British approached with Rimington's Scouts ranging ahead, Boer fire made it evident that the previous night's Boer complement had been reinforced. The Northamptons and the Northumberland Fusiliers formed the left while the Naval Brigade, with the King's Own Yorkshire Light Infantry in support, went for the easternmost kopje, a high, steep, rocky prominence, to the right of the original line of advance which pointed due north and converged on the railway. Lieutenant W. T. C. Jones of B Company, Royal Marine Light Infantry wrote:

'Not quite certain why this movement was taking place, for only the commanding officers knew exactly what we were intended to do, we trudged along through the coarse grass, keeping our left shoulders well up to avoid the ugly rocky kopjes in our immediate front. The sun was beginning to be very hot and we were becoming somewhat "droopy", as no one had had any breakfast … and we had been marching already for three hours and a half…

'We glanced at the kopjes and almost wondered why the guns poured such a tempest of shrapnel over them; rarely did we catch sight of a figure moving among the rocks, and with the exception of the enemy's guns on their right, vigorously replying to our own, the whole position looked harmless and untenanted.

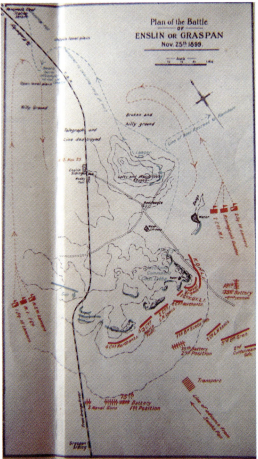

Above **Erected here in error and with a mistaken inscription, a monument to the Royal Naval Brigade stood at the roadside facing the Graspan kopjes.** (MFME BW13/16)

Left **A plan of the Graspan engagement from** *The Times History.* (TM. MFME BW3/18)

Below **Diagram of a shrapnel shell from W. F. Stevenson's** *Wounds in War.* **A time fuse on the nose ignites the charge at the base of the shell, throwing the shrapnel forward.**

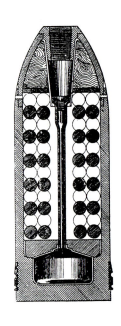

'At 7.45 we were some seven hundred yards from the base of the isolated kopje on the Boer left, and the field battery ceased firing. Almost immediately from the rocks, which a moment before seemed lifeless, there opened the wild crackle of Mausers.'

The bluejackets and marines turned to face the fire and went in at the 'quick'. Men started to fall. An optimistic and archaic order was given: 'Volleys! Ready! Present! Fire!' but the futility of the procedure was immediately evident and independent fire took over. They had started this attack from about 700 yards (640m) from the base of the hill and between 500 and 200 yards out the earth was boiling with rifle fire, not only from the kopje ahead, but also from the left flank where Boers ousted from the hill to the north had come down to the scrub in the centre of the horseshoe of kopjes and were supporting their left. Here the Naval Brigade received the majority of its casualties. The foot of the hill gave some respite, sheltered as it was from the left and too close under the positions on the hill for fire to bear. The KOYLI rushed across the fire zone on their right and, bayonets fixed, up they went. Resistance soon faded as the Boers once again took to their horses and rode away.

Meanwhile the 12-pdrs., two of them, under Lieutenant F. W. Dean of HMS *Monarch*, were involved in a duel with the Boer guns on the northern hills. He had been ordered by the Royal Artillery officer in command to withdraw, but could not do so without risking his men because they had too few mules to move the guns fast enough on their makeshift carriages. So they stayed. Dean wrote:

'I therefore continued to fire as briskly as possible at the Boer guns, with such effect that we continuously put them out of action for as much as fifteen or twenty minutes at a time. Their shells burst with the utmost accuracy, and both our guns and ammunition trolley were spattered all over with shrapnel balls; but owing to my system of making all hands lie down when we saw their guns flash, and remain till the shell burst and the balls flew by, we had only six men wounded [out of 50], when, at 9.30am the Boers finally ceased firing and abandoned their position.'

The limited effect of shrapnel is illustrated here. The shell was a hollow cylinder with a timing device at its nose, a charge at the base, and a mass of metal balls in between. The timer ignites the charge which bursts the casing and throws the balls forward, the speed imparted by that of the shell being augmented by the force of the charge. You now have a large number of bullets flying forward in an expanding cone. Against men under cover, it is useless. Against men in the open, assuming the timer is correctly set, it works a treat. The attempt to use shrapnel to soften up Boer positions on rock-covered hills and in sangars was, it can be seen, futile.

The Marines lost two officers and nine men killed and one officer and 72 men wounded out of a force of five officers and 190 men, while the bluejackets lost two officers and two men killed and one officer and five men wounded. The Marines' casualties, at 44 per cent, were heavy. Methuen said they had attacked in too close formation and Jones suggested that as the kopje was 'peak-shaped' it was possible that everyone took the summit as the line, and so got drawn close together.

The cavalry, once again, could do little to mop up the retreating Boers who were moving off in good order with their guns and their wagons. The 9th Lancers had been away on the left, close to the railway, waiting their chance and the New South Wales Lancers were with them. Trooper Peter McDonald was with a group that was counter-attacked. He wrote:

'We had a dangerous go for it. The Major of Mounted Infantry to which we were attached, said to us: "Come boys, let us die together." So we took up a firm stand, but there was just a handful of us. We ran up on the brow of a hill, and sent our horses away under Henry Robson to a place of cover. We fired on the Boers who were trying to cut us off, dropping several of them from their saddles. Of course we held a good position or we would never have stood. However we turned about 500 Boers and never lost a man.'

Methuen was annoyed at a second failure of the cavalry and dismissed the commander of the 9th Lancers, Lieutenant-colonel B. Gough. This was scarcely just, given the quality of the horses and the lack of mounted troops. Gough shot himself.

Above **At this stage of the war British uniforms were not fully modified. The officer of the Highland Light Infantry still wears trews, the private of the Argyll and Sutherland Highlanders has a kilt cover that leaves his rear view conspicuous and the dead Grenadier drew attention to himself by the coloured hackle on his helmet.**
(Gerry Embleton, from Men-at-Arms 303 *Boer Wars (2) 1898–1902*)

It now appeared that the next major obstacle to overcome this side of Kimberley was the complex of hills of Magersfontein and Spytfontein, immediately south of the town. Between the British and those positions of strength the railway crossed the Modder River just west of its confluence with the Riet River. The peninsula between the two streams was known as Twee Rivier. Here grew tall trees and here stood the Island Hotel, playground of Kimberley, where many a lazy Sunday afternoon had passed in pleasant dalliance. To this pleasing spot the British advanced.

MODDER RIVER

The station master at Modder River was helpful. He informed the British that the Boers had blown the railway bridge and were in occupation of the north bank and reconnaissance by the 9th Lancers and by Rimington's Scouts put their number somewhere between 'thousands' to the Scouts' figure of 400 men. This led Methuen to abandon his idea of making a great encircling foray to the east; the Modder had to be secured here first.

The scouting left a good deal to be desired. So did the map. Methuen had a sketch headed *Modder River*

Left **The KOYLI Memorial. The Modder River bridge lies beyond the trees behind the memorial.** (MFME BW14/14)

Right **The infantry pinned down at Modder River. They have managed to dig in to some extent with their entrenching tools.** (NAM 6902-10-1)

Below **The Gordon Highlanders prepare to advance at Magersfontein. The kilted troops suffered fearfully from sunburn when prone under enemy fire, having no protection for the backs of their legs.** (McG.)

Railway Bridge and dated 19 October 1899 made by
Captain O'Meara, but this was drawn from memory
alone and failed to show the course of the Riet
southwards on the British right or the resort of
Rosmead with its dam on the British left. The title of
the sketch suggests it was never intended to do more
than show the bridge, but the commentary was
misleading as Methuen's annotations show. To what
extent conditions had changed with the different
season, as it was presumably reconnoitred in winter, is
hard to say. What no map could tell Methuen was the
plan developed by Koos De la Rey.

The Boers had been dismayed by the losses
sustained at Belmont and Graspan. True, the British
losses had been greater, but the Boers fought to live
rather than to die; dying was for the professionals.
Taking position on hill-tops had not proved
satisfactory. The plunging fire of their rifles failed to
make the most of the Mauser's flat trajectory; indeed,
the Naval Brigade had suffered most when enfiladed
by fire from men who had descended from their
kopje. Finally the smokeless powder in use would
allow them to take up positions which might be

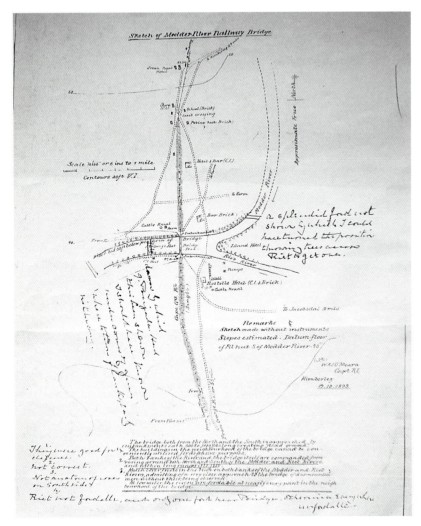

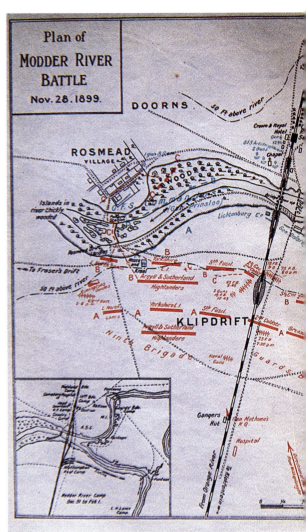

vulnerable if known, but were secure when undetected. De la Rey persuaded Cronje and Prinsloo that they should entrench on the southern bank of the river with fall-back positions ready dug on the northern bank. The artillery was less cunningly arranged. There were four 75mm guns to the north-west of the bridge but the rest was on Twee Rivier or south at Bosman's Drift, the first ford on the Riet where it crosses the Free State border.

Against a frontal attack the Boers were excellently arrayed, and a frontal attack is what Methuen gave them. At 4.30am on Tuesday 28 November the British moved forward. On the left was the 9th Brigade under Major-general R. Pole-Carew with the 1st Loyal North Lancashires, the 2nd King's Own Yorkshire Light Infantry and the 1st Northumberland Fusiliers with the newly arrived 1st Argyll and Sutherland

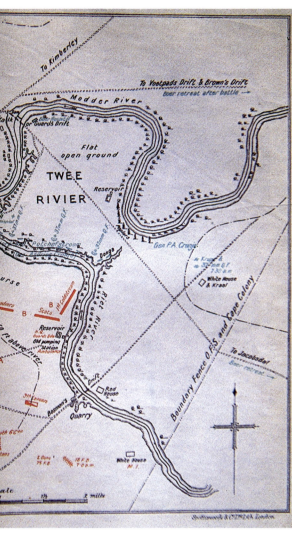

Above **Plan of the Modder River action from** *The Times History.* (TM. MFME BW3/19)

Left **The Guards Memorial with, shown by the line of trees in the distance, the course of the Riet River.** (MFME BW14/17)

Below **Map of the country between the Modder River and Kimberley by Claude Lucas, Government Surveyor. It is based on farm surveys, surveys by Major O'Meara, RE and on general information gleaned from reliable sources. It is undated, but is certainly not earlier than 1 April 1900 as O'Meara was promoted to the rank of Major on that date.** (RE5201.8.9. MFME BW18/30)

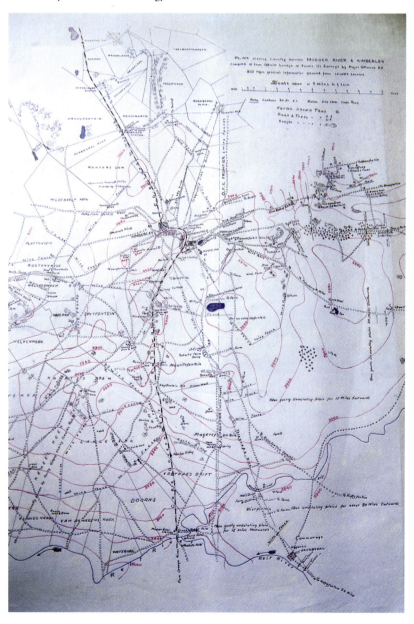

Highlanders in reserve while the Northamptons were in the rear, guarding the camp. On the right was the Guards Brigade, the 2nd Coldstream, 3rd Grenadiers, 1st Scots and the 1st Coldstream in reserve. The artillery in support of the 9th was the naval battery of 12-pdrs., on a low crest some 4,800 yards (4.4km) from the Modder. The 18th Field Battery was on the railway and 75th Field Battery was with the Guards. An hour after starting the infantry was approaching the Modder crossing, and there was not a sign of the enemy to be seen.

Methuen was up with the troops as they came down the gentle slope towards the river and remarked to Major-general Sir Henry Colvile, commander of the Guards Brigade, that the Boers were not there. Colvile responded that if they were they were sitting tight when, at some 1,000 yards (910m) from the Modder, the Boers opened up. Immediately the British hit the dirt. Colvile tried to have the 1st Coldstream work round the right flank but they stumbled up against the unexpected Riet River, and though they worked along the left bank for some way they were soon pinned down like everyone else. And there they had to stay, baked by the sun, steadily becoming more and more thirsty, bitten by ants and shot if they raised themselves above a totally prone position. The artillery attempted to engage the Boer guns with some success, but the Free State Artillery commander, Major Albrecht, had prepared alternative positions for his pieces and moved them about to confuse his adversaries.

On the left the 9th was similarly stuck, except that they could see some of their enemies in a clutch of farm buildings on the near bank forward of the hamlet of Rosmead. Here, after midday, the Argylls managed to insinuate themselves along a gulley and cut the Boer front line. The Free Staters were worried by this and their fire slackened. The KOYLI then charged the farm and ejected the Free Staters who fell back across the river by way of a drift and the dam to Rosmead. Pole-Carew followed with some of the Loyal North Lancashires and Argylls. He sent for reinforcements, but got very few. The 62nd Battery, which had come all the way from the Orange River that day and had to cut dead horses from their traces

on the way, was able to add its efforts to the 9th's, but by now Methuen was wounded and Colvile in command. Communication failed and Pole-Carew stood where he was, Rosmead in his hands and De la Rey's Transvaalers blocking further progress.

As darkness came on the Free Staters drifted quietly away. De la Rey was willing to hold on, but Cronje, his senior, was for withdrawal. By dawn on Wednesday the Boers were gone. The Modder was crossed without another shot fired. It had cost Methuen 70 dead and over 400 wounded, while the Boers suffered about 50 killed and an unknown number wounded. And now they were positioned, or so it seemed, on the hills ten miles south of Kimberley, ready to fight again.

MAGERSFONTEIN

The British assumed, and their scouting did nothing to disabuse them, that the Boers would adhere to their standard practice and occupy the high ground. De la Rey thought differently, and managed to persuade his

Left **The Modder River from the south bank, looking along the line of the old road and drift towards Modder River Station. The railway bridge is now higher and wider than the original.** (MFME BW13/29)

Below **Magersfontein seen from the Scandinavian Memorial crosses.** (MFME BW14/7)

Bottom **In the grass and scrub below the hill, rocks reveal the line of the Boer trenches.** (MFME BW14/9)

Right **The Boer positions near Magersfontein, mapped by No. 1 Survey Section shortly after the Boers withdrew in February 1900. The map was logged into the Intelligence Division, War Office, Map Room on 10 July 1900. After the battle in December the defenders of this line extended and improved their trenches, but held the same line.** (BL E54:10[35])

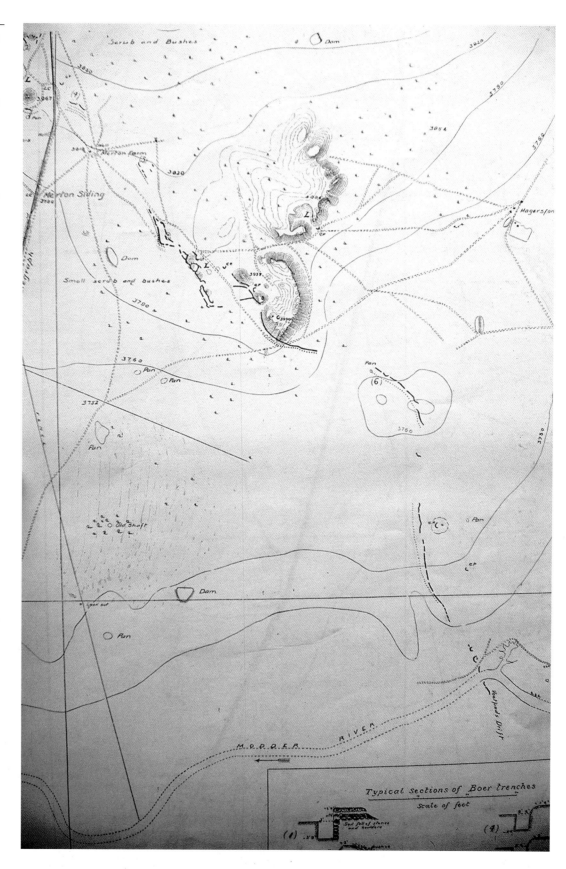

colleagues, Cronje and Prinsloo, of the validity of his approach. What the Modder River had demonstrated was the effectiveness of Mauser fire over a plain. The dangerous zone of rifle fire was increased. The Boer position should therefore be at the foot of the range of hills. Accordingly a long trench was dug, some three feet (1m) deep with a stone breastwork and further fortifications placed on the flanks so that a line from west of the railway to Voetpads Drift on the Modder River opposed the British. From the heights of the Magersfontein kopjes themselves the view of the Modder River Station is almost uninterrupted, except for a trivial hummock known as Horse Artillery Hill and a scarcely perceptible ridge they called Headquarters Hill, and Kimberley is in clear view in the other direction.

Methuen's problem was the lack of information. The Boer position ran from north-west to south-east across the railway, along the Magersfontein sector, across the Kimberley road and, along a ridge, down to the Modder River. The British were pinned to the railway with a desert to the west and an unknown Boer presence to the east. On 6 December a Free State force had attacked at Enslin, on the railway south of the Modder River, and only a determined resistance by the Northamptons had prevented the cutting of communications; it might happen again. The

Magersfontein line was, in addition, the last point of resistance the Boers could take up this side of Kimberley. The orders Methuen issued stated:

'It is intention of GOC to hold enemy on north, and to deliver an attack on the southern end of Magersfontein ridge … On the afternoon of 10th December the position will be bombarded; it will be assaulted on the 11th. With this end in view three columns will be formed.'

It was thus to be another frontal attack, along an axis south-west to north-east, with Pole-Carew's 9th Brigade holding the western flank and the 2nd KOYLI keeping an eye on the river to the east. It was decided to use the newly arrived Highland Brigade under Major-general A. G. Wauchope in the centre accompanied by the 9th Lancers and Mounted Infantry to cover the right flank with the Guards in reserve. The approach would be by night march, probably less for the achievement of surprise than for the use of darkness as cover in the open country to the south of the Magersfontein ridge. Indeed, the decision to shell the supposed Boer positions on 10 December cannot be reconciled to a tactic of surprise and the concentration of fire on Magersfontein itself was an open declaration of intent. An attack next day and against this position was a certainty. The shelling itself was futile. First, it was directed on the wrong targets, the heights, and second the Boers sensibly stayed under cover; only three wounded were reported.

Wauchope himself appeared to be less than confident about the night march. The evening of 10 December found the Highland Brigade behind Headquarters Hill and, at a half hour after midnight, they started forward arranged one company behind another in mass of quarter columns, a solid block of men some 42 yards (32m) wide and 170 yards (155m) long. The 2nd Black Watch came first, followed by

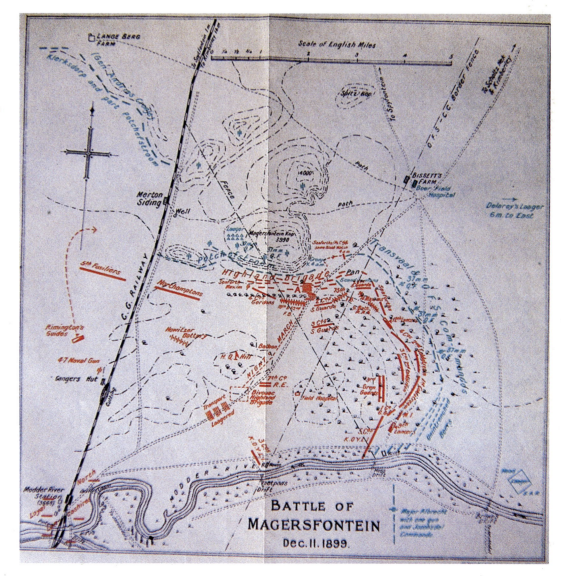

2nd Seaforth Highlanders, 1st Argyll and Sutherland Highlanders and finally 1st Highland Light Infantry. It was pitch dark and stormy. Captain J. H. Bruche, a Victorian Special Service Officer, was with the Highlanders.

'The rain was so heavy that it rather helped the column, the approach of which otherwise might have been betrayed by a lightning flash… There was a vague sense of being one of a large body of men without proof of it. There was not a sound except the one instruction whispered over and over again … "No loading without orders until daylight. Only the bayonet to be used." Wire fences - not barbed wire - had to be dealt with …'

The ground was open to observation in daylight, but full of traps at night; stones and anthills conspired with scrub to trip and delay. Their guide, Major G. E. Benson, managed, in spite of the conditions, to get them close to the desired position by 3.30am, half an hour late, but this was still short of the start line for the attack by close on half a mile (750m) and too far west as well. But it was close to dawn and Benson advised deployment into the extended attack formation. Wauchope disagreed. Not only did he order the men forwards once more, but he also changed the mode of deployment, from 'to the left', to 'left and right', sending the Argylls to the right and the Seaforths to the left of the Black Watch. It was now nearly 4am. They were about 400 yards (370m) from the undetected trenches and dealing with a patch of mimosa thorn. A Company of the Black Watch had deployed and B Company was in the process of doing so, the rest were still in mass of quarter column. The Boers opened fire. Bruche said:

'The Boers' opening fire came as a continuous roar for about half a minute, then followed a slight pause, broken by a repetition of the roar. Each roar marked the emptying of the Boers' Mauser magazines, the slight pause the time taken to insert more clips of cartridges.'

The Black Watch at once attempted to charge but were halted by the massive weight of fire. Those in the rear could not bring their rifles to bear. Wauchope was aware that the fire was less intense to the right, where the road passes round south-east of the hill, and had given the order to extend to the right when he was killed. Lieutenant-colonel Coode received the order but was himself struck down before he could act or pass it on. In the confusion the Highlanders struggled to deploy as best they could before being pinned down to fry in the unforgiving sunshine of the summer day. On a little hillock forward of the Orange Free State lines on the ridge to the east, a Scandinavian volunteer unit was slaughtered by the Scots. To the south-west of the crosses that preserve their memory, on Horse Artillery Hill, G Battery, Royal Horse Artillery and the 9th Lancers were stopped by rifle fire, but unlimbered and came into action. The recoil shoved them back down the slope, out of the storm of Mauser bullets, and thus able to sustain fire on Boer lines. Here they were joined by 75th Battery which assumed the task of the Magersfontein target leaving G Battery to continue its bombardment of the eastern ridge. The position of the guns was not in accordance with text-book practice of the time and the battery commander was subsequently rebuked. The text-book has since been changed.

The day passed in probe and counter-probe along the eastern flank as the Guards and Cronje sought each other's weakness. None was found. On the eastern slopes of Magersfontein small parties of Highlanders managed to mount attacks, only to be shot down, taken prisoner or, on at least one occasion, caught by their own artillery. Early in the afternoon The Boers started to outflank the Seaforths on their right and the subsequent movement exposed them to fire. The Gordons, who had been sent forward in a near suicidal attack mid-morning, also moved, during which manoeuvre their commanding officer was killed. Control was lost and the movement turning into a flight as, for the first time that day, Boer

Right **On 19 December the body of General Wauchope was reburied at Matjesfontein, near Beaufort West, in a plot donated by brother Scot the Hon. J. D. Logan. Eleven officers and 195 other ranks formed the escort.** (A. J. McKechnie Coll. MFME BW17/16)

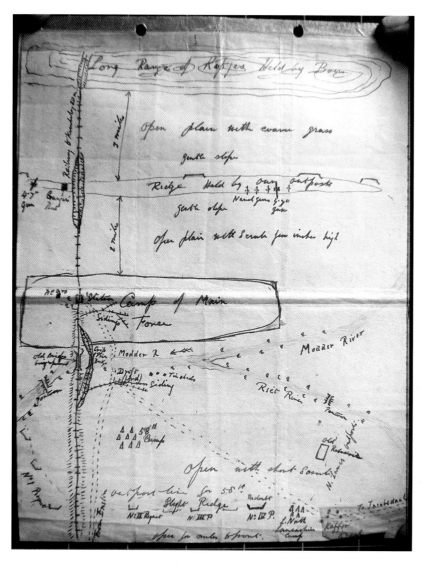

Above **Barton's sketch of the front line before Magersfontein where the British were to stay until Lord Roberts arrived.** (NRA. MFME BW19/15)

artillery opened up. The Highlanders ran and Methuen had to throw the Scots Guards in to plug the gap.

Private James Williamson, of A Company, 2nd Black Watch, wrote from hospital at Netley, near Southampton, of his experience.

'We … got no command off any one, only had to charge on our own tinpot way, and to my sorry I was in the front Company, we pulled up the barb wire and rushed on the Boers but were soon away from them again, we extended out to the left and lay down … the Bullets were coming down like hailstones so we had to stick there, about 30 yards [27m] from the trenches, as soon as I lay down I got a Mauser Bullet through my left foot which made me wilder so I started firing back but my luck was out that day, for they peppered at me as if I was the only man firing at them. I got one through the left leg severing my mussle then I got another in the back but kept on the fire as long as I was able to hold the Rifle, then I got one in the right shoulder, it made me drop the rifle but I managed to pick it up and fire again, but not for long for

I got another in the right leg so I thought it was the last, but no I got another in the right arm that broke it …'

It had taken six wounds to end Williamson's fight, but then he had to lie there throughout the day and all the following night. At about 9am the Boers allowed three men of the Highland Light Infantry to come over for him.

Lieutenant Barton, with the Northamptons, saw little of the day's events.

'We, E Coy, moved out about 5 [am] & remained lying down in the plains … we advanced occasionally, the 5th Fusiliers being on our left / the other side of the railway / early in the afternoon we drew near the first of the Kopjies but saw no enemy … During the whole day our Artillery shelled the hills with Lydite & shrapnel … it was very hot lying all day on the open Veldt …'

As darkness fell the Highlanders, some virtually ordered to do so by the Boers, trailed back. A knot of Guards and artillery stayed on until the next day around Horse Artillery Hill and a truce to attend the wounded was arranged for the morning of 12 December. The British casualties approached 1,000, of whom 210 were killed. Three-quarters of the casualties were from the Highland Brigade; it is no wonder the Scots object to the conflict being called the Anglo-Boer War.

The Boer losses were, perhaps, 87 killed and about 170 wounded, but it is hard to be precise with an informal force. Methuen withdrew to and fortified Headquarters Ridge while Cronje's men extended and deepened their trench system to produce the substantial works that appear in the old photographs.

Barton wrote two days after the battle:

'Dec 13th, Wednesday. Construction of earth-works commenced upon the hill or ridge lined till then by outposts …'

And there they stood. There were minor forays. Barton records being in support of the Highlanders, he does not specify the regiment, who were themselves supporting the artillery on a reconnaisance in force on the afternoon of Wednesday 17 January, 1900. Little came of it, but Barton was shaken by the way the Highlanders carried themselves as the party withdrew to camp.

'… they came back utterly disorganized like sheep scattered over the plain without shepherds … Poor Highlanders I am very sorry for them, Magersfontein has no doubt broken their spirit & they will take many years to recover from the shock.'

He was not wildly complimentary about his own men. Ordered to advance in the shelter of the raised river bank,

'… the men, with the usual stupidity of the British soldier for warfare requiring wary & cautious movement are inclined to walk along the top of the bank and offer themselves against the skyline to any concealed Boers & with difficulty they are got to follow in Indian file well

apart and far enough from the edge of the bank to just see the other side without exposing their bodies ...'

Five days later the Northamptons received orders for 47 men and two officers to go to Orange River to join the mounted infantry regiments that were being formed. Barton lacked the skills of horsemanship required.

'I am disappointed beyond all words for everything points to our remaining here maybe for months not only doing no active service but with absolutely nothing to do but eat & sleep here in camp day after day, the effects of which lazy life are telling on me terribly so that it is quite an exertion to get up & go to the river to bathe.'

Poor Barton was to be stuck there for quite some time.

THE CENTRAL FRONT

While Major-general Sir John French had secured the Cape Colony border and railway lines at Naauwpoort Junction, the Orange Free State invasion further east on the East London railway line through Stormberg had led to the occupation of that junction by the Boers. Lieutenant-general Sir William Gatacre decided they should be removed, although he had been ordered by Buller to act with caution.

Most of Gatacre's division had been posted to Natal, leaving him seriously undermanned. He had acquired, by the start of December, three new battalions, 300 Regular Mounted Infantry, 1,000 Cape Volunteers and two batteries. He then felt strong enough to go for Stormberg. A robust and tireless man, he seriously underestimated the impact of forced marches on troops. What is more, Stormberg had been occupied, before Buller had given the order to withdraw, by 2nd Royal Berkshire Regiment. Indeed, the fortifications of the place were their work, but in spite of their knowledge of the ground Gatacre left them behind, and chose to take the 2nd Royal Irish Rifles and 2nd Northumberland Fusiliers, together with his mounted infantry and the guns. These troops were moved to Molteno, some ten miles (16km) south-east of Stormberg, which lies in a valley with the Kissieberg ridge to the south-west and Rooi Kop to the east. A night march was to put them in a position to take the ridge from the Boers at dawn.

The entire operation was mismanaged. Gatacre either changed the route and failed to tell the supporting troops or his guides got lost. The route was not properly reconnoitred. In any case, the main body went needlessly westwards, lengthening the march considerably, while the ammunition and hospital trains followed the northward road. Gatacre's column actually passed the place they wished to attack, but as the guides had not been informed of the objective and as Gatacre himself mistook his position, they went on. Dawn of 10 December found them marching through a pass where the Boers, in classic position on the heights above, opened fire. The Irish Rifles managed to scale the hill but the Northumberlands were faced with a cliff they could not surmount. They managed to withdraw and the order was given to fall back on Molteno which they did with losses of 25 killed and 110 wounded, only to discover that they had left nearly 600 men behind to become prisoners.

COLENSO

By this time Buller had devised his approach to attacking the Tugela line, where the river wound its way beneath the towering kopjes to present a moat and a wall for the Boers to oppose the relief of Ladysmith. His artillery had been augmented by

Right **Tethered against recoil, No.2 4.7in. gun fires on the Boers.** (McM. MFME BW10/20)

Below **Map of the Colenso action from** *The Times History*. **The marking of the Boer positions omits the artillery on the slopes above Vertrek (Robinson's) where the 'V' in the hill is still lined with emplacements, and on the road north-west from Colenso, now the main Ladysmith road, just short of the zig-zag. The presence of Boer forces on Nhlangwini (Hlangwane) gets a passing note. Whether these deficiencies arise from ignorance or from the book's editor's, Leo Amery's, dislike of Buller can only be guessed.** (TM. MFME BW3/23)

Captain Scott's mobile 4.7ins., another masterpiece of improvisation. After HMS *Powerful* had left with the fixed-mount guns he had turned his attention to designing a gun carriage. Some 4in. (10cm) square bar iron was found in a blacksmith's shop and, to a design sketched on the spot, work began. Some 4ft (1.22m) diameter circular plate was located which, with the addition of angle iron to form a tyre, became wheels. A wooden trail completed the carriage, and the first was ready in 48 hours. These were the guns that Scott had taken to Durban and which Buller now took,

together with 16 naval 12-pdrs., to Colenso, served by sailors from HMS *Terrible*.

Buller's initial plan was to outflank the Boer force on the hills north of Colenso, for the approach to the river from the south was across flat, open land. This he could see for himself, and he lacked any more detailed map than a five-inch to the mile school map. He intended to hold the Boers here with a demonstration by Major-general Barton's 6th Brigade while he made a night march to Potgieter's Drift, a ford some 18 miles (29km) upstream overlooked by Spioenkop from the north-west and Vaalkrans from the north-east. Between the two there was a road to Ladysmith. The march was planned to start on 12 December. Then Buller got cold feet. The Boers had just scored notable victories at Magersfontein and Stormberg and both Methuen and Gatacre were at the end of long, vulnerable supply lines, as, indeed, was Buller himself. If he made a foray so far from the railway, might not the Boers cut him off? He sent a message to Lord Lansdowne:

'... *I cannot think I ought now to take such a risk. From my point of view, it would be better to lose Ladysmith altogether than to throw open Natal to the enemy.*'

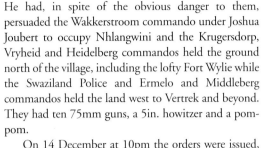

Right **The positions of Long's guns, looking east from the bridge over the railway close to Colenso station. The modern embankment of the spur line to the power station is on the left and the red brick buildings of the sewage farm are to the right. Under the power lines is the relic of the donga in which the gunners sheltered and the gun positions are shown with yellow blocks. In the distance to the left is Nhlangwini.** (MFME BW9/25)

Below **A Boer gun position still exists within a couple of minutes' walk from the main Ladysmith road, north-west of Colenso beyond the turning for Pieters. From it the tall trees now marking the Loop of the Tugela River are clear to see.** (MFME BW9/17)

The frontal attack on Colenso would be undertaken, in spite of Buller's previous misgivings.

Quite how detailed Buller's understanding of the terrain was is difficult to establish. What is evident from the ridge south of Colenso village is that, to the west, the river meanders on the far side of a gentle slope, kissing the foot of the hill behind Vertrek farm which rises to Red Hill. West of north stands Grobbelaarskop and between these hills the main road to Ladysmith. The railway line crossed the river north of the village and ran between the Colenso Koppies and the western bank before making its convoluted way to Ladysmith on a route now largely abandoned. This is where it got hard to see the land clearly. Some two miles (3km) north of Colenso the river turns eastwards, passing north of the Nhlangwini, or Hlangwane, ridge and, further east, the height of Monte Christo. It is not clear if the British were fully aware of the topography in this latter sector and the importance of Nhlangwini on the Boer flank. That there were still local people in the area is evident from the report of a farmer, one Pringle, rescuing an ammunition wagon after the fight and the apparent unwillingness to quiz those who knew the area is a puzzle.

Louis Botha was now in command of the Boer defence, and he had banked on Buller attacking here.

He had, in spite of the obvious danger to them, persuaded the Wakkerstroom commando under Joshua Joubert to occupy Nhlangwini and the Krugersdorp, Vryheid and Heidelberg commandos held the ground north of the village, including the lofty Fort Wylie while the Swaziland Police and Ermelo and Middleberg commandos held the land west to Vertrek and beyond. They had ten 75mm guns, a 5in. howitzer and a pom-pom.

On 14 December at 10pm the orders were issued, too late to reconnoitre the ground. Major-general A. F. Hart's 5th (Irish) Brigade would advance on the left, the west, to cross the Tugela at Bridle Drift, to the west of a great meander known today as 'The Loop', and to turn back eastwards to roll up the Boer line. Major-general H. J. T. Hildyard's 2nd (English) Brigade was tasked with taking Colenso village itself and then, reaching the far bank of the river by way of two drifts and the Ladysmith road that left, and still leaves, over a bridge that now bears Buller's name, attacking the Colenso Koppies. Meanwhile, on the right, Colonel Lord Dundonald's Mounted Brigade was to attack Nhlangwini. Colonel Long's 14th and 66th Field Batteries and Lieutenant Ogilvy's naval guns would be on the right and Colonel Parsons's 63rd and 64th Field Batteries on the left where Major-general N. Lyttleton's 4th Brigade was in support. Major-general G. Barton was in command of the supporting 6th Brigade on the right.

Hart's Brigade were given some bracing drill before moving off at about 4am. Hildyard's were not so quick off the mark, and Long's artillery, which started at 3.30 as ordered, was soon racing far ahead of the infantry. At 5.30 the 4.7in. guns and four 12-pdrs. under Commander Limpus began shelling the heights beyond the river from a position west of the railway. For three-quarters of an hour the bombardment continued without reply from the Boers. On Hart's left the 1st Royal Dragoons saw the Boers across the river and sent warning to the General who decided to treat them with disdain. The closer Hart got to the Tugela the more his brigade drifted eastwards. His African guide pointed him into The Loop, while others warned him he was entering a salient. Leaving the 1st Scottish Borderers to hold the bank on the west, he led the 1st Connaught Rangers, 2nd Royal Dublin Fusiliers and the 1st Royal Inniskilling Fusiliers on into a certain disaster. Hart liked to keep his troops under his close control and they marched on in mass of quarter columns, the formation that had proved so costly at Magersfontein.

Meanwhile Colonel Long had made swift progress and found himself east of the village, where today the redundant power station blocks the view to the north beyond an embanked railway siding and where a sewage farm stands to the south. The Boers were silent. Long remarked that they had fled. Lieutenant F. C. A. Ogilvy was with him.

'About 6am … I was riding in front with Colonel Long about 450 yards [410m] from Colenso station, when he directed Colonel Hunt to bring his guns into action just in front of a deep donga running across our front at right angles to the railway. He then told me to come into action on the left … In front of us was a line of trees up to which our skirmishers had advanced, also a few artillery outposts. Just as I was about to direct my guns where to go, and as the Royal Artillery were unlimbering, the outposts turned sharply and a murderous fire, both rifle and shell, was opened on the guns and ammunition column.'

Ogilvy went back and found only two of his guns had crossed the donga safely before the oxen had scattered, so with two guns forward and two in the rear, he engaged Fort Wylie while efforts were made to get the remaining two guns out of the donga. He noticed that as the Royal Artillery men were shot down, replacements were sent forward from the ammunition column by a sergeant, but after about half an hour their fire ceased. Lack of men, lack of ammunition and Boer fire had persuaded them to shelter in the donga, taking the wounded Long with them.

On the left Hart was now enduring the crushing, scything fire of Mauser and Krupp, or, to be precise,

the Irish Brigade were while, apparently bearing a charmed life, the General himself strode about unharmed, pushing his men deeper into trouble and even preventing the Iniskillings from creeping out on the left and attempting the river closer to the correct place. Trooper T. Sulivan, the Queenslander who had so much impressed Hildyard at Estcourt, was attached to the Irish that day.

'We found the Boers entrenched on the banks of the River Tugela. As we approached they opened a withering fire on our brigade, so the order was given to swim the river and in we jumped. I left my horse behind and joined the rush. To our surprise we found the Boer entrenchments surrounded by barbed wire, so we set to work to cut a gap in the fence. We were all but through when the Boer cannon opened on us and the order was given to retire. While I was cutting my last bit of wire a shell hit the iron post on my right, and took the head clean off a Connaught Ranger. Then I though it might be my turn next so I got back to the bank …'

From the height of Vertrek, from a gun emplacement on the Ladysmith road and from trenches on the north bank, the Boers poured an unrelenting fire on the Irish.

Away on the right Dundonald had dismounted his men to attempt an assault on Nhlangwini. Joubert's men held them and appeals to Barton for support went unheeded. Only in the centre did things go more according to plan where Hildyard's men, advancing in open order and by bounds, using cover, occupied Colenso without much trouble but were then required

Above **The bright green farmland within the tree-lined Loop is dominated by the old gun position on Vertrek, south-east of Red Hill. The principal Boer trenches were on the north-eastern side of the Loop, where open water can be seen. The cooling towers in the distance are near the station in Colenso and close to Long's position.** (MFME BW9/37)

Left **Long's abandoned guns were taken in triumph to Pretoria before being taken into service with the Boers.** (McM. MFME BW12/10)

Far Left **A contemporary photograph illustrates the extensive Boer positions on the Tugela Heights.** (RE23/377. MFME BW18/17)

Left **Ted Clouston with a wheel from Long's troop. What could not be taken was thrown in the river by the Boers and recovered by the farmers on their return.** (MFME BW10/2)

to cover the attempt to save Long's guns. And on everyone the sun blazed down, completing the exhaustion that the fighting had started.

Buller ordered Lyttleton to extract Hart from the trap in which he had entwined himself and Hildyard to cover the mission for the guns, while the Commander-in-Chief himself rode off to extract Long's guns. He found Ogilvy who reported that he

'... rode up and directed me to move our guns and ammunition as soon as I could. The guns were got away each by a team of artillery horses, who galloped them up the hill to the rear. The waggons were far more difficult, owing to their weight, the large circle they required to turn in, and to the fact that they had to be got out of the drift and turned round by the guns' crews before the horses could be put on. About this time a most brilliant feat was performed by two teams of artillery, who galloped to the front, against a most murderous fire, limbered up, and rescued two guns; a similar attempt by one other team, at least, resulted in the entire team, as far as I could see, being destroyed.'

Among those who had ridden out to retrieve the guns were members of Buller's and Clery's staff, including Lieutenant Freddy Roberts, son of Field marshal Roberts, Captain Schofield and Captain Congreve. The saving of, and attempts to save, the guns led to the award of four Victoria Crosses, one of which went to the dead Lt. Roberts. Buller ordered these efforts to cease and the remaining guns were abandoned to the Boers.

Eversley Belfield quotes Louis Botha as saying:

'... it was Colonel Long who ... realized our force on Hlangwani [Nhlangwini] was already across the river and there was grave danger of a flank attack, and he made it so hot that they had to open fire all along and so gave the whole plan away ... They blamed him for the failure, but that man saved the British Army that day.'

The argument about the wisdom of Long's actions that day will not easily be settled. The cost of the

attempt to retrieve the guns shows that trying to supply them with fresh ammunition and bring them into action again, as Belfield contends was possible, would also have failed.

By 7am the general order to retire was given and the British struggled to extract themselves, in daylight and without significant covering fire, from their positions. Some managed it in three hours, others took all day and yet others were still out there when evening came and the Boers crept over the river to take them prisoner. Buller had lost seven officers and 138 men killed, 43 officers and 719 men wounded and another 220 missing or taken prisoner; remarkably trivial numbers by the standard of later wars or the American Civil War, but enough to convince those at home in Britain that this was the third massive disaster of 'Black Week'.

Even before the battle, moves had been made in London to replace Buller with Roberts, and now that decision was taken. Buller wrote to his wife.

'Just as I was writing to you an unpleasant surprise has supervened. A telegram has come to say that Lord Roberts is appointed C-in-C, and I am relegated to command in Natal. I have expected this. Two days after I arrived here they ordered me to supersede Sir George White, and I would not, they then later ordered me to supesede Gatacre and I would not, and then Methuen and I would not, so now they have superseded me. I honestly confess I am not sorry ...'

Serving with the Boers was Colonel J. Y. F. Blake, Commander of the Irish Brigade. After the war he wrote:

'The Boers generally acknowledge General Buller as by far the ablest commander the English had in the field. True it is, he made mistakes on the Tugela, but ... had [he] been in supreme command, I firmly believe the war would have been brought to an end within six months after the relief of Ladysmith.'

RELIEF!

While Methuen and Buller had been making their ponderous progress to failure, Ladysmith, Kimberley and Mafeking had remained under siege. The force in Ladysmith was substantial and in no mood to sit supine and wait for help. Early on the Boer shelling had, inevitably, hit the Town Hall and endangered the hospital area. General White arranged a truce with General Joubert for the removal of civilians and wounded to a camp south of the town and Nurse Driver made preparations for the move.

'On going into Spark's shop for a big hat, I was surprised to see a major in charge. He said I could take some necessary things and that he would like to see what I took to make a note of it. I looked happily round the shop. After finding half a dozen aprons for myself … I thought how very useful a big man's mackintosh would be… During those many nights at Intombi this was to be the most used and treasured garment we had.'

On 5 November the train took doctors, nurses and patients out to the open Veldt where a few tents had been erected.

'There was of course no platform as yet. We climbed down halfway and then gave a big jump, only to be confronted by a barbed wire fence… We scrambled through and looked about us in this wilderness… In a dip that looked as if it would be under water in a storm,

they had pitched two bell tents and a marquee very badly.'

The arrangements were hurried and poorly carried out. It was two full days before any reasonable standard of comfort had been created and never were the conditions to approach anything better than makeshift. Here they treated the wounded to begin with and, later, the victims of enteric (typhoid) fever.

The citizens of Ladysmith were, at first, fascinated by the whole business of being besieged. Bella Craw went with her uncle and aunt to look around on 12 November, after Sunday lunch.

'[We] went for a ride, up the ziz-zag road to Caesar's Hill. Men are camped all over it… We were riding comfortably along, when we saw a man following us. We

Above right **The graveyard at Intombe, with the modern railway and the height of Caesar's Camp beyond. The hospital is shown on the other side of the railway on the old Ladysmith map, and the graves are about where the road on that map ends, but now have to be approached on this side of the rails from a point in Ladysmith itself.** (MFME BW7/1)

Right **Intombi Camp, No. 12 Field Hospital, established by agreement as a neutral zone. In the distance is the great bulk of Mbulwana (Umbulwana) with Lombard's Kop to the left and Gun Hill further left.** (TM. Photo Henry Kisch. MFME BW4/23)

saw he was a Staff Officer by the red on his collar… [He] told us Colonel Hamilton did not wish us to go any further as he did not feel it was safe. He also said the very ground we were riding over last Thursday was covered with Boers and bullets were as thick as bees.'

Deneys Reitz was at Bell's Kop, north of the town. He settled down and managed to make himself comfortable.

'Our boy Charley proved a capable freebooter, and thanks to his foraging expeditions into the hills among the Zulu kraals where he made play with his descent from Chief Mosesh, our larder flourished and our mess was the envy of the rest of the camp. After a week or two, tents were served out, and my brother and I shared one with the five good friends of our corporalship with whom we had kept company ever since leaving home… they were all killed before long.'

A defensive perimeter was established. The town itself runs south-west to north-east in the space between the Klip River and Convent Hill, with a clutch of hills extending to the north-west. Small hills stand to the east and west of the town itself, while to the south the terrain is more open with, first, the hump of Maiden Castle and beyond it the great slab of the Platrand made up of Caesar's Camp and, at its western end and separated by a saddle, Wagon Hill. An attack mounted from anywhere other than the south would have to overcome a succession of hills, each made into a strongpoint, while an attack from the south would encounter the serious obstacle of Caesar's Camp. White had every reason to be optimistic about holding out until help came. Indeed, he had a good jumping-off point for aggressive action.

The Boers were also content with their dispositions. To the north, on Pepworth, they had a Long Tom and west of that they occupied Bell's Kop and Surprise Hill. Further on, on the Harrismith road, the Free Staters had a camp and hospital at Smith's Crossing and round to the south the little hills each had their marksmen at the ready and often an artillery piece. South-east, on the height of Mbulwana, was another Long Tom and north of that, on Gun Hill, forward of Lombard's Kop, due east of the town, they

had not only a Long Tom, but two 75mm guns and two howitzers.

Although shelling continued on a daily basis, boredom became a real enemy. Major G. F. Tatham reported that, on 29 November,

'General order issued to stand to arms at 2am. This order was countermanded in consequence of its having become too generally known. No one knows what was to have been done, all were anxious for action and gladly received order to move and regretted contrary order.'

He was to get satisfaction on the night of 7–8 December.

Left **Major Bruce, RAMC, in Ladysmith using 'the X-Rays' to locate a bullet in a wounded man's arm.** (TM. Kisch. MFME BW4/24)

Below left **A list of passwords for use by the Boers investing Ladysmith, 14 to 31 January, 1900.** (Graham Jacobsen Coll. Photo M. & C. French)

Bottom **Huts in the Zulu style housed Boers on the Klip River at Nelthorpe on the Pieters road.** (McM. MFME BW10/30)

MAP OF
THE SIEGE
OF
LADYSMITH

'General [Sir A.] Hunter came to [Colonel W.] Royston during the afternoon [of 7 December] and arranged about Gun Hill attack. He, in command, took 650 of following:-'

the Natal Carbineers, Border Mounted Rifles and Natal Police, under Colonel Royston, and the Imperial Light Horse under Colonel A. H. Edwards. Captain G. H. Fowke commanded the men of the Royal Engineers. They were led off at 11pm by Major D. Henderson with a small group of the Corps of Guides. General Hunter himself commanded the centre in the advance up Gun Hill. Arthur Crosby was with the Natal Carbineers.

'The first intimation of what was going on was when we came up to the I. L. Horse, who were lying by the road. One of the men told me that 100 each of their men and Carbineers had to take the guns (which had been teasing us for the last month) on Gun Hill … As we approached the Dutch lines we moved along very cautiously, and our walk was then reduced to creeping and crawling… Gained the bottom of Gun Hill … about 1.30 … Here we laid down ready loaded for an

Left **A map of Ladysmith, made and published in London, but giving a fair impression of the topography and of troop dispositions.** (McM. MFME BWMF8)

Right **A sketch map made by Captain G. M. Heath, Royal Engineers, from the observation balloon on 18 November 1899. The attempt to identify and mark Boer positions is admirable but disappointing. It appears that the sketch is pierced and perhaps it had pins stuck in to show where the Boer guns were.** (RE5201.33. MFME BW18/27)

Below left **The Oval, Ladysmith, from Convent Hill with the blunt tower of the Town Hall on the far side, beyond a mass of parked wagons, and the Platrand in the distance.** (McM. MFME BW10/34)

Below right **Today the Oval is a shopping precinct. The top of the Town Hall tower can still be seen and the car park is in the same place as the wagon park. The Convent is now a hospital from which it is possible to walk down to the graffiti marking a 12-pdr. emplacement.** (MFME BW8/16)

attack, within an hour we heard a Dutchman challenging our men 3 times, "Wie Kom daar" (Who comes there), and then a shot, followed by a terrific roar. Cheer upon cheer … 3 distinct explosions followed, a party of some 20 Royal Engineers having blown up the two guns.'

Colonel Edwards and Major Karri Davies had shouted 'Fix bayonets' despite the ILH's lack of them, and the few defenders of the summit had fled. The Long Tom and the howitzer were blown up and a

Maxim and the sights and breech-block of the Creusot taken. For a cost of one man killed and five wounded, according to Crosby, a very satisfactory sortie.

Three days later another sortie was made, this time by 2nd Rifle Brigade and a dozen Sappers under Lieutenant R. Digby-Jones. Reitz was out on picquet duty with a small group of Pretorians from their base at Bell's Kop at about 1am.

'After a while I distinctly heard the muffled sound of many footsteps in the direction of Surprise Hill … We

Above **Boers under canvas behind Lombard's Kop.** (McM. MFME BW11/20)

Below right **Cattle roam next to the remains of the fortifications on Wagon Hill.** (MFME BW7/34)

withdraw. Reitz's little band had, in the meantime, made its way to the foot of the hill from which Tossel and his men had fled. There they were challenged twice and twice opened fire on the picquets the British had left to guard their line of retreat.

'As we were going, a soldier, lying concealed in the grass on the bank above us, thrust over the muzzle of his rifle, and fired point-blank into us. My tent-mate Samuel van Zijl was walking immediately in front of me and I had my hand on his shoulder to steady myself on the uneven path. The bullet struck him full in the throat, and so near was the range that the discharge scorched his face, and set fire to his beard, which flared up for a moment like a fusee.'

Samuel fell, still alive, and Deneys made him as comfortable as he could. The little group then took up position facing the hill, backs to Ladysmith, and listened as the triumphant riflemen scampered down towards them. They waited. Then, in the gloom, they saw a solid body of men approaching. At the order they opened fire,

'shooting as fast as we could work the bolts of our rifles. When the blast struck them they thought they were being fired at by their own rearguard pickets, for there were cries of "Rifle Brigade! Rifle Brigade, don't fire!" but, discovering their error, a commanding voice called out, "Bayonets, Bayonets," and they came at us like a wall.'

The charging riflemen passed to one side of the Boers and were away into the night. More British came down the hill, some to be shot, others taken prisoner and still more to escape, inflicting casualties on the Pretorians as they went. Fifteen men died and

thought Corporal Tossel's men [posted at the foot of the hill] had taken fright at something, and were withdrawing up the slope towards the howitzer emplacement. This belief was rudely dispelled, for suddenly there broke from the summit … a crash of musketry … a vivid sheet of flame stabbed the darkness, followed by a tremendous roar, and we knew that our howitzer had been blown into the air.'*

Digby-Jones had been obliged to return to the gun after the first fuse had failed, but the gun was then destroyed and the Rifles could attempt to

Left **British soldiers built themselves shelters of stone and corrugated iron against Boer bombardment.** (McM. MFME BW11/23)

Below **Memorials to Lieutenant Digby-Jones and Field Cornet De Villiers stand side by side on Wagon Hill.** (MFME BW7/29)

another 60 or so were wounded or prisoner on the British side and the Boers admitted to four dead, seven wounded and the loss of one gun.

The next substantial attack from the town was planned for 14 December, with over half the garrison involved. The scheme was abandoned on receipt of the news of Buller's failure at Colenso.

Dr James Kay had volunteered to serve at Ladysmith, leaving his family in Howick to which they had fled from Pretoria in September. He took a break from Intombi hospital on 25 December.

'On Christmas Day I left by train, on leave from 5pm until … morning … Went to the back of the Standard Bank, opposite the Royal Hotel, and in a very large room Karri Davies, Col. Frank Rhodes [Cecil's brother], Royston and others had decorated the room very nicely and there were four Christmas trees labelled, "Canada", "Australia", Britain" and "South Africa". At 7pm all the children in Ladysmith were to be there …

'… That very morning the gun on Bulwana fired two shots, the shells pitching in town without exploding. When dug up, they were found to be stuffed with rough plum pudding and outside on the shell was painted "A Merry Christmas"… Subsequent shelling dispelled … favourable thoughts …'

Early in the New Year the Boers mounted their only serious attack on the Ladysmith defences. Commandant C. J. de Villiers with the Harrismith commando and General Prinsloo's Free Staters had originally planned an assault on the Platrand, which dominated the southern approaches to the town, at

the end of November. Indeed, the Pretorians had actually launched the feint on the other side of town against Red Fort, as Reitz names their objective. Now, on 6 January, a more substantial attack was to go ahead. The Transvaal men under Schalk Burger numbered 1,000 and were to go for Caesar's Camp. De Villiers would lead the Free Staters, 400 of them, against Wagon Point while 600 from the Vryheid, Winburg and German commandos would be in the centre. Not all of the latter turned up. The Long Toms on Mbulwana and Telegraph Hill would bombard the British fortifications. These were serious structures with walls seven feet (2m) high, built on the northern edge of the plateau with gun emplacements for 42nd Battery, Royal Field Artillery in between and picquets on the forward edge of the hilltop.

For all this the hill was not usually strongly manned. The Manchester Regiment held Caesar's Camp together with a party from HMS *Powerful* and the Natal Naval Volunteers with a 12-pdr., and the Imperial Light Horse and three companies of 1st King's Royal Rifle Corps held Wagon Hill, with 600 men in total. But work was in hand on Wagon Hill to build two new gun emplacements and Lieutenant Digby-Jones of the Royal Engineers was there with a team for that purpose. Further, a detachment of Natal Naval Volunteers with a 3-pdr. Hotchkiss had arrived the previous day and two naval guns, a 4.7in. and a

12-pdr. were coming up that night. The Gordon Highlanders had provided a guard for this party. At 2.30am De Villiers hit Wagon Hill. Surprise was complete and the occupants fell back at first, but rallied quickly, finding cover in sangars and gun-pits. In the dark flashes of rifle fire could be friend or enemy, all was confusion as little groups of combatants struggled against each other and Boers swarmed over the hill-top. Colonel Ian Hamilton had his headquarters near the Manchesters on Caesar's Camp. Woken by the noise, he used the newly-installed telephone to contact General White for reinforcements and, with two companies of Gordons under Major Miller-Wallnut, set off along the Platrand towards Wagon Hill. Here he met Colonel

Above **From the Devons' memorial the broken ground over which they attacked is easily seen, but the Boer positions are obscured by scrub.** (MFME BW7.36)

Above right **Evidence of the presence of the Natal Naval Volunteers on the Platrand, the location of their galley.** (MFME BW7/11)

Left **The Boer Memorial, Platrand. The fallen both from actions around Ladysmith and those further afield have been gathered for burial here.** (MFME BW7/10)

Right **The ruins of Cove Redoubt, looking out over what was Tin Town and is now the army camp, towards King's Post.** (MFME BW8/23)

Edwards with three companies of Imperial Light Horse and four of Gordon Highlanders, sadly without their Commanding Officer, Colonel Dick-Cunyngham, who had been mortally wounded by a stray bullet as they came. The Gordons were sent to reinforce the Manchesters. The ILH went for Wagon Hill.

Meanwhile the Transvaalers had climbed the eastern end of the Platrand, insufficiently fortified, and taken the Manchesters on the flank. The progress of the Boers was challenged by the Natal Volunteers and halted by the bayonet charge of the Gordon Highlanders who regained the lost ground. The artillery, 53rd Battery, now it was light, turned its fire on the attackers from a position east of Maiden Castle and attracted counter-fire from the Long Tom on Mbulwana, which in turn was fired on by the 4.7in. at Cove Redoubt. At about 8am six companies of the 2nd Rifle Brigade reached Caesar's Camp and seized the position on the eastern summit, although they

Above **Men of the Natal Naval Volunteers, looking remarkably like Boers with their Martinis and *agterryer* or after-rider, at Caesar's Camp.** (McM. MFME BW11/6)

Left **The Naval 4.7in. gun of HMS *Powerful* at Cove Redoubt.** (TM. Kisch. MFME BW4/5)

Right **Lady Anne Battery with a 4.7in. of HMS *Powerful*.** (TM. Kisch. MFME BW4/6)

lacked any precise orders to do so. The GOC, Hamilton, was elsewhere.

The fighting at Wagon Hill had appeared to have slackened and Hamilton was at the 4.7in. gun pit when the Free Staters under Field Cornets Jacob de Villiers and Zacharias de Jagers renewed their attack. Hamilton himself was present when the confused fight took place. Accounts vary, but it appears that De Villiers shot Major Miller-Wallnut dead just as Trooper Albrecht of the ILH was shooting De Villiers. Albrecht was immediately killed by De Jagers who was at once struck down by Digby-Jones who himself was killed immmediately after. The Navy counter-attacked to secure the position. Hamilton did not lack for courage, but he could scarcely be in command of his whole force in these circumstances. For the next four hours the fighting continued and further reinforcements clambered up from Ladysmith to lie in the long grass and try to see a target.

Between Wagon Hill and Wagon Point to the west there is a small nek, little more than a pinch in the sides of the hill and a dip in the crest-line. Here a party of Free Staters had established itself, pushing up to a line of rocks that enabled it to fire freely across the hill top to the east and west. White had drawn off almost the last of the troops he could afford to put onto the Platrand before holes appeared elsewhere in the perimeter. At 4pm Lieutenant-colonel C. W. Park received orders to take every possible man of the Devonshire Regiment across Ladysmith and to report to Colonel Hamilton. Park arrived an hour later with five officers and 184 men, soaking wet as a result of a ferocious thunderstorm. Hamilton explained the position – there were the Boers and they could not be shifted. The only way was a bayonet charge. Could Park do it? Park wrote to his wife afterwards:

'Of course, I could only answer that we would try… We fixed bayonets and charged magazines, and I explained to each company [there were three] exactly what we had to do, and when all was ready Colonel Hamilton said, "Go on, and God Bless you", and away we went, the men cheering and shouting for all they were worth. The first few yards we were under cover, but when we reached the top of the crest line we were met by the most **awful** storm of bullets. I have never heard such a hot fire in my life … The little ridge of rocks which the Boers held was right in front of us, and between us and it was 130 yards [119m] of open flat grass without the smallest cover or shelter of any kind. The men behaved splendidly; every man went as straight and hard as he could …'

As they ran the men fell on every side. The sight was too much for the Boers, they ran before they were caught. The Devons took cover in the position just vacated but were still under heavy fire. Lieutenant J. Masterson ran through the thick of the fire to take Park's message to the ILH to ask for relieving fire. The Devons hung on until it was dark, wet through, many wounded, increasingly and debilitatingly cold, until, as night fell, the last of the Boers could be heard abandoning the hill. The cost of holding the Platrand had been 17 officers and 158 men killed of a total casualty list of 424. Five Victoria Crosses were won that day, by Privates Pitts and Scott of the Manchesters, Masterson of the Devons and two were awarded posthumously, to Albrecht and to Digby-Jones. The cost of the Boer attempt to take it had probably been as heavy. Neither side had the advantage in courage.

The next day Arthur Crosby made the mistake of going to take a look.

'I made for the scene of the recent fight which took me close upon an hour, the hill being so precipitous and with huge boulders which made the climb most difficult. On reaching the crest a ghastly sight presented itself. Two of the enemy's dead (one a German) were lying just where

I landed. Both had been killed by shrapnel and horribly mutilated. Walking round a radius of about 100 yds. I saw some 25 more … As nearly all had been killed here yesterday morning, they were in a shocking state of decomposition …'

A Boer burial party was approaching under a white flag, and Crosby found himself told off to help gather up the dead and carry them down the hill to their comrades. They had no stretchers, so they used the wheelbarrows the Manchesters had needed for moving stone, their belts, their puttees, anything they could find to carry the shattered, rotting bodies down for burial. The Boers made no further attempt to take Ladysmith.

In the following weeks sickness and hunger beset the besieged. The price of the commonest commodities soared. Morale was at a nadir and then got worse. Eyes scanned the hills to the south, beyond which Buller, apparently, was doing nothing.

KIMBERLEY

The investment of Kimberley started on 14 October 1899. The great diamond town was, as the result of dubious legal manoeuvring, in Cape Colony rather than the Orange Free State and therefore Milner had taken an interest in its security before the war. Lieutenant-colonel Robert Kekewich was asked to inspect the place and, when he declared it vulnerable in the extreme, to do something about it. For this purpose he had half of his own battalion, the 1st Loyal North Lancashires and a half dozen 2.5in. guns. They arrived in late September 1899.

The energy with which Kekewich set about fortifying the town was such that, only three weeks later, the Boers found themselves obliged to lay siege to Kimberley. Trenches had been dug, mine waste tips converted into redoubts and volunteers raised. There was no shortage of labour; thousands of African mineworkers were housed in compounds belonging to De Beers. Guns and ammunition were also contributed by the mining company, which should not, of course, have had them at all. Left over from preparations for the Jameson Raid were 422 rifles, six machine-guns and 700,000 rounds of ammunition. Soon the defenders of Kimberley numbered 596 regular soldiers, 352 Cape Police and some 5,500 volunteer Town Guards. The enterprising American engineer employed by De Beers, George Labram of Detroit, designed and built a conning tower on the winding gear of De Beers principal mine from which, 115 feet (35m) up, Kekewich could oversee operations and speak to his outposts by telephone. Even when the Boers started shelling on 6 November the main interest appeared to be the collection of shell fragments for sale.

Perhaps more than by the enemy, Kekewich was troubled by Cecil Rhodes. The mining magnate became worried about the 10,000 African workers, seeing them as a threat to the populace, and attempted to send 3,000 Basutos back to their homelands. The

Below **The proud creators of Long Cecil gather round the finished gun. Its designer, George Labram, has a proprietorial hand on the muzzle.** (McG. MMKP1342)

Right **The Long Tom blown up on Gun Hill, outside Ladysmith, was taken to the Transvaal for repair. The barrel was shortened and, nicknamed 'The Jew', it was brought back into service against Kimberley.** (McM. MFME BW11/4)

Below **Boer positions on Carter's Ridge, outside Kimberley.** (McG. MMKP1499.)

Right **The Memorial to the Honoured Dead in Kimberley is adorned with the famous gun, Long Cecil.** (MFME BW14/20)

Far right **The Memorial also carries a plaque in memory of the American engineer, George Labram.** (MFME BW14/23)

Boers drove them back towards town where they were fired on by the garrison who had not been informed. Rhodes had no hesitation in communicating direct with Milner and Buller and demanding military action that was either absurd or impossible. At the same time he was to place the resources of De Beers in the service of the people of the town, both in offering shelter from shelling and in keeping people fed.

In November the British sought to support Methuen's advance with a little diversionary action at Kimberley. A number of sorties were undertaken, of increasing scale, under Major Scott-Turner. On 25 November it was Carter's Ridge, to the south-west, that they attacked, suffering seven killed and 25 wounded, but capturing over 30 Boers and killing or wounding a couple of dozen more. Rhodes viewed these efforts with contempt and taxed Kekewich with cowardice in failing to try a break-out to join hands with Methuen. The foray against Carter's Ridge did not stop the shelling from that position and Scott-Turner determined to try again to silence those guns. This time, on 27 November, the defences were more

robust. Two dozen of the British died, Scott-Turner among them, and another 32 were wounded. Rhodes was quick to accuse Kekewich of incompetence.

The greatest crisis occurred in February 1900, long after the advance had been stopped at Magersfontein and before the arrival of Field marshal Roberts appeared to be bearing fruit. Since 19 January the Boers had been enduring British shelling of a serious nature. The amazing Labram had designed and built a 4in. gun in the workshops of De Beers and with this weapon the first real threat was made to the Boer gun emplacements around the town. Olivier d'Etchegoyen was a Lieutenant in a foreign unit sent to Kimberley, arriving on Tuesday, 6 February, with a Long Tom. This was the Creusot that had been blown up on Gun Hill outside Ladysmith, repaired and restored in somewhat shortened form. It had lost some inches off the barrel, and was known as 'The Jew'. The Frenchman Colonel Georges Compte de Villebois-Mareuil and his comrade the Austrian Baron de Sternberg greeted the new arrivals. They were obviously a little unpopular for they had been

Above **The siege-soup kitchen at De Beers' Convict Station. Cecil Rhodes is sitting next to Mrs Rochefort Maguire, the lady in white.** (McG. MMKP4301)

Right **The Long Tom is laid for fire on Mafeking.** (McM. MFME BW12/5)

expected two days earlier, and for two days in succession Villebois-Mareuil 'had had good luncheons prepared. Then, having given us up, he had ordered nothing, and we took his kitchen by surprise.'

Having joined the forces of General du Toit, they took their gun to Kampferdam, where a wooden platform to carry the gun was constructed and the efforts to mount it went on all night. On Wednesday morning the first shot was fired into Kimberley. Over the next four days the shelling of the town caused more damage than had been done in all the weeks since October and the population went in fear. Labram himself was killed on the Friday, changing for dinner in his hotel room. Women and children were offered shelter in the mines.

As the siege wore on food became a problem and supplies of all kinds were short. By the end of it the suffering of the black population, restricted to an inadequate diet, had reached so great a pitch that 483 of them had died of scurvy. Nine civilians and 42 officers and men lost their lives besides.

MAFEKING

The little town of Mafeking on the border of the Bechuanaland Protectorate, of which it was the administrative capital although it was in Cape Colony, had a population of about 1,700 whites and 5,000 black Africans, most of them Barolong in the adjoining settlement of Mafikeng. In September 1899 it had been discounted as a defensible position by the authorities in Cape Town and its only hope lay in the forces in the north. There Colonel R. S. S. Baden-Powell had organised the Protectorate Regiment, under Lieutenant-colonel C. O. Hore, based north of Mafeking in the Protectorate, and the Rhodesia Regiment under Colonel Herbert Plumer, the latter based in Bulawayo. The recruiting was carried out in secret.

In terms of inflicting damage on the British, besieging Mafeking appears a rather mistaken gambit on the part of the Boers, but it was hoped that it would lead to an uprising of Dutchmen in Cape Colony and, possibly even more important, it had symbolic significance as it was the starting point for the Jameson Raid.

By the end of August it was clear that the supplies accumulating in Mafeking were in need of a guard as the Boer forces in the area were reported variously as being between 5,000 and 20,000 men. On 19 September Baden-Powell moved the Protectorate Regiment into Mafeking with Colonel C. B. Vyvyan as Base Commandant; he had the men where he wanted them in a well-victualled and defensible place. His guns were not up to much, he had received two muzzle-loading 7-pdrs. instead of the howitzers he asked for, and he had far too few men, a mere 20

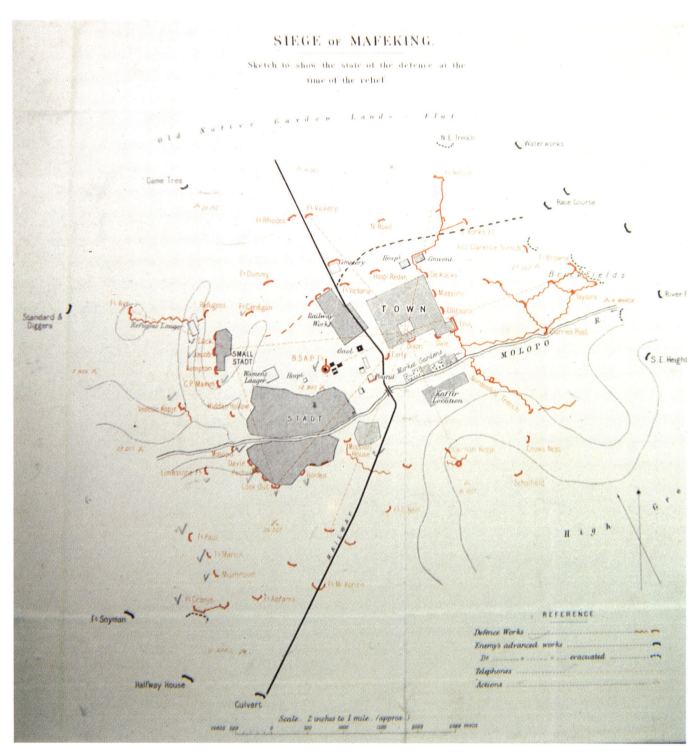

SIEGE of MAFEKING.

Sketch to show the state of the defence at the
time of the relief

Above **A plan of Mafeking
showing the layout of
fortifications at the end of the
siege.** (RE5201.16/7. MFME BW19/0)

officers and 680 men, including police. To this were
added the Town Guards, somewhat reluctant citizens
numbering, perhaps, 300 who complained that they
had to do all the work. With this force Baden-Powell
succeeded in holding the town. Delicacy, tact and
diplomacy were irrelevant; an iron determination and
a strong streak of stubborness were needed, as well as
a large portion of luck. Plus a willingness to make use
of the loyal and courageous Baralong, a feature of the

siege not admitted afterwards even by Baden-Powell
himself – some 750 of them were armed (Baden-
Powell admitted to 300) and known as the 'Black
Watch'.

In the circumstances deception was to prove a key
contributor to success. The building of fortifications
was undertaken with great energy, two defensive areas
being defined, the Exterior embracing the native *stadt*,
Mafikeng, to the south-west on the other side of the

railway tracks from the European town, with the southernmost point at Cannon Kopje and a series of forts covering the western approaches astride the Malopo River. The Interior area was the European town itself, protected on the west by the British South Africa Police fort and on the north by the armoured train on its siding. Major Alick Godley, Adjutant of the Protectorates, commanded the western defences and Colonel Vyvyan the Interior.

There was still hope of acquiring more guns, but this was dashed when, on 12 October, De la Rey cut the railway line at Kraaipan, 35 miles (55km) south of Mafeking, and attacked the train transporting the weapons – the first action of the war. Not only were the guns lost, but also the armoured train, one of two he had, that Baden-Powell had sent to fetch them. The next day Boers were seen from Cannon Kopje and the other train was sent out to prevent them settling in too close. On 14 October Lord Charles Cavendish-Bentinck was sent out with A Squadron of the Protectorates to investigate what was happening to the north, and very nearly got caught in a trap as the canny Boers retreated to ensnare him. Baden-Powell had to send out a reserve squadron under Captain Charles FitzClarence only to learn that he too was yielding to the temptation to pursue the Boers too closely. Out went the mighty train and an order to FitzClarence to withdraw to prevent disaster, but a benefit was the impression of British strength and confidence given to the Boers.

General Piet Cronje brought up his Creusot on 24 October. The shelling from the 75mm guns had been going on for some days, unpleasant but relatively harmless in a spread-out township. Now serious damage would be done. The next day a Boer attack on the *stadt* was thrown back, mainly by the armed Baralong, and Baden-Powell decided a counter offensive was necessary. On the night of 26 October FitzClarence led an attack on the trenches closest to the town, to the north-east. The result was unsatisfactory, surprise was not achieved and a decision to use only the bayonet reduced Boer casualties to, perhaps, three killed and some wounded while the British lost six dead and nine wounded as well as two missing. On 31 October a determined attack was launched against Cannon Kopje which was defended by 45 British South Africa Police commanded by Colonel J. A. Walford. Some 700 Boers came from the south and a second group from the south-west. The shell-fire on the fort continued unrelentingly as the Boers came on and it seemed certain that they must succeed. It was the gunnery of Lieutenant K. Murchison that turned the tide. With two puny 7-pdrs. and remarkable accuracy the attackers were put to flight.

As the days passed Cronje came to the conclusion that his energies were better spent elsewhere. The

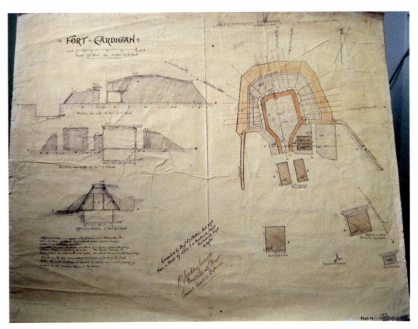

shelling continued, but the British seemed to be set solid and able to resist direct attacks. A force of 2,000 men under J. P. Snyman was left to continue the siege. Inside the town life was boring and unpleasant. Drunkenness became a serious problem, and one officer had to be relieved of his duties because of his habitual inebriation. The daily bombardment did not kill many, but in a population of 1,700 white civilians and 700 soldiers, the eventual loss of 115 killed was considerable, and almost everyone would know nearly all of the slain. Amongst the Africans the causes of death are not categorised, so the total of about 700 includes those who died of disease or starvation. Baden-Powell stands accused of deliberate witholding of food from the Africans, but this is hard to sustain in the light of recent research. In the latter stages of the siege disease became a serious problem, particularly of the very young and very old, and thus had a greater impact on the black population. Even so the figures speak for themselves; the death rate amongst the Europeans was half of that of the Africans.

The physical destruction accumulated until, as Filson Young of the *Manchester Guardian* reported when at last he was able to enter the town,

'As one passed house after house, one with a gaping hole in its side, another with the chimneys overthrown, and another with a whole wall stove in, none with its windows completely glazed, all bearing some mark of war - as this panorama of destruction unfolded itself one marvelled that anyone should have lived through the siege.'

There was little Baden-Powell could do about it. He had no artillery that could hurt the Boer emplacements. Careful sniping scored modest victories and a ship's gun a century old was found being used as a gatepost and pressed into service.

Above **Fort Cardigan, a major fortification to the west of the European town. Drawing by Sergeant F. J. Stebbins, Protectorate Regiment, after a sketch by Lord Charles Cavendish Bentinck.**
(RE5201.16/2. MFME BW19/3)

Below The Pont, or floating bridge, at Potgieter's Drift.
(LSM. MFME BW6/24)

Although it had 'B.P. & Co.' marked on it, it was dubbed Lord Nelson and fired solid shot at the enemy. Good for morale, but little else. It was frustration that led the defenders into a foray with fatal consequences. North of the town the Boers had dug trenches known to the British as Game Tree Fort. They were assumed to be open trenches, no one recalling that, as Baden-Powell himself had noted on 17 November, they had been roofed with corrugated iron and covered with earth.

Just before daybreak on 26 December 150 men attacked this stronghold. The armoured train was out in support together with three 7-pdrs. and two Maxims and a further 100 men were in reserve with another gun. It was costly and unsuccessful, with 26 killed and as many again wounded or captured. The Boers suffered 13 casualties, three fatal. Three Victoria Crosses were won that morning, one awarded to FitzClarence. Nothing like it was tried again. From then until the relief in May 1900 survival was the objective and survival alone.

BULLER'S LEFT HOOK

South of the Tugela, early in January, just as Lord Roberts was arriving at Cape Town, Sir Redvers Buller was reinforced with Lieutenant-general Sir Charles Warren's 5th Division and decided to go back to his original plan, an advance on Ladysmith by way of Potgieter's Drift. On 10 January they made a start, a train of 650 wagons, 25,000 men and the Navy's great guns together with eight field batteries. Sir Frederick Treves, surgeon to the Queen, followed on 13 January with the hospital train of 16 ox wagons and five mule-drawn ambulances, a small covered wagon, a Scotch cart and a mounted guide. They got to Spearman's, the new headquarters, three days later. And while the endless columns plodded along, the Boers shadowed them from the heights of the hills north of the river.

From the foot of Mount Alice the road runs north-east over Potgieter's Drift, along the eastern flank of a great meander of the Tugela and up the shallow pass of Brakfontein before curving eastwards over the plain to Ladysmith. To the right of the road the heights of Kranskloof culminate in Vaalkrans, beyond another meander in the river which takes on the aspect of the head of a crumpled bulldog with two erect, chewed ears, looking down to Colenso to the east. To the left of the road, which passes between the ears, the undulating heights of Twin Peaks climb towards Spioenkop, which with Conical Hill and Twin Peaks, makes an arrow pointing south-west. Further left again the line of the Ntabamnyama heights streches north-west to terminate in Bastion Hill near Acton Homes on the Ladysmith to Bergville road (see map on p.79). Today the terrain is harder to relate to Buller's time because of the huge lake, Spioenkopdam, that obscures the river west of Trichardt's Drift.

The vanguard of this great migration of the British was formed by Dundonald's Mounted Brigade, splashing ahead of the mired-down infantry. They were on Mount Alice on 11 January. It took Buller two days to make up his mind what to do next. It was not until 17 January that the British started to cross the river. Buller gave Warren the left, crossing at Trichardt's Drift, and Lyttleton the right, a holding action, beyond Potgieter's Drift. The latter was secured on the 16th. Warren was to cross the Ntabamnyama hills while Lyttleton kept the Boers busy, but it would be necessary to move quickly. Dundonald hurried off to the west and reached Acton Homes easily on 18 January. Warren recalled him, deeming the flank too long. It was an opportunity lost. Meanwhile Warren's division filed across the river and camped on the northern side, while the Boers busied themselves digging trenches above.

Left **Boer look-outs on Conical Hill.** (McM. MFME BW11/31)

Below left **Troops crossing a pontoon bridge at Trichardt's Drift.** (LSM07/881. MFME BW6/19)

Below **Artillery thrusting up the steep bank from the pontoon at Trichardt's Drift.** (McM. MFME BW12/3)

Finally, on 20 January, an attack on Ntabamnyama took place to secure the road that now approaches Spioenkop by Roseleigh, the way one comes from Ladysmith today. Dundonald took Bastion Hill, but Hart and Woodgate, in the centre and on the right, found themselves on a false crest, facing another, well-fortified, summit which they could not overcome given the perfect field of fire the sloping plateau gave the Boers. After two days they were still in the same place. Buller visited Warren on the 23rd, which did not please the latter, to push him either to advance or withdraw. The decision was made to take the hill the other side of the road, Spioenkop, so as to be able to bring artillery fire to bear on Ntabamnyama. Given that the objective is a hill that rises steeply on all sides, the scheme to use it as an artillery platform seems far-fetched, and it may well be that no one had a clear objective at all, action driving out thought.

The operation started at 11pm that same night. Major-general E. R. P. Woodgate led men from the

2nd Lancashire Fusiliers, 2nd King's Own Royal Lancasters and the South Lancashires from his own Lancashire Brigade, 1,700 in all, together with 200 men of Thorneycroft's Mounted Infantry, dismounted for this affair, and some Royal Engineers. To follow were a mountain battery, artillery and machine-guns. The column was led up the steep slope by Colonel Alec Thorneycroft. One of his troopers, the Australian R. L. Nicholls, recalled:

'In some places we had to climb on hands and knees, in others we had to clasp hands and help each other as well as we could.'

A challenge when they reached the top was followed by a fusillade before the little picquet of Boers fled, leaving one of their number dead to a bayonet thrust.

Now the task was to entrench, but the true shape of the supposed summit was unknown and in the dark impossible to determine. Moreover, the ground was rocky in the extreme and digging out of the question. They therefore raised what breastworks they could from the loose stone on the surface and waited

Above **The Boers fought from the very edge of the steep northern side of the hill, sheltering amongst these rocks. Conical Hill is in the background.** (MFME BW5/23)

for dawn. When it came fog prevented a proper evaluation of their position at first, but a brief lifting of the murk showed they were too far south and east, so they moved forward to the edge of the hill-top and attempted to build again. Louis Botha, made aware by the fleeing burghers that the hill was occupied, made provision for the artillery to be ready to open fire with daylight.

Deneys Reitz and his companions of the Pretoria commando had been sent from Ladysmith to reinforce the men on the Tugela line. In the night they heard the sound of rifle fire and with the morning were summoned to help.

'Heavy shells were lobbing over as we went, but we had not far to go and in less than fifteen minutes had reached the bottom of Spion Kop. Here stood hundreds of saddled horses in long rows, and we looked up at an arresting sight.

'The Boer counter-attack had started shortly before. Eight or nine hundred riflemen were climbing up the steep side of the hill in face of a close-range fire from the English troops... Many of our men dropped, but already

Below **The Spioenkop hills seen from the Boer, the northern, side. From the left the hills of Twin Peaks punctuate their ridge which rises to Spioenkop itself, with Aloe Knoll on the left, lower than the main mass of the hill. A ridge leads right to Conical Hill, beyond which a nek divides it from the flat-topped Green Hill and the main ridge of Ntabamnyama. The Twin Peak and Conical Hill ridges are at right angles, forming an arrow-head of which the spur on the opposite side of Spioenkop is the point.** (MFME BW4/38)

Above **Mass graves in the main trench on the summit of Spioenkop. On the left trees grow amongst the rocks that formed the Boer line after they had pushed the British back. On the right the summits of Twin Peaks and, closer, the tops of trees on Aloe Knoll.** (MFME BW5/15)

Above **The British camp below Ntabamnyama.** (LSM07/882. MFME BW6/23)

Right **British ambulancemen searching for survivors. The rifle-carrying Boers are said, in the original caption, to be looting, but may just as well have been seeking their fallen.** (McM. MFME BW11/26)

the foremost were within a few yards of the rocky edge which marked the crest, and soldiers were rising from behind their cover to meet the final rush. For a moment or two there was confused hand-to-hand fighting, then the combatants surged over the rim and on to the plateau beyond where we could no longer see them.'

Reitz and the Pretorians then started up the slope, steep though, on this side, not very high. As they climbed they passed dead and wounded men they knew. Once at the top they saw that the Boers had managed to gain a lodgement in the boulders that surround the summit, but had got no further. Having been delayed by meeting his brother, Reitz attempted to rejoin his commando which had been sent off to the left. He found the stones suddenly stopped, as they still do today, and was unable to follow them across the gap which was now closely watched. He returned to the shelter of the firing-line that faced the trenches near the modern memorial, the trenches that afterwards became mass graves.

'The English troops lay so near that one could have tossed a biscuit among them, and while the losses which they were causing us were only too evident, we on our side did not know we were inflicting even greater damage upon them.'

And there Reitz stayed all day, without water or food, in constant danger, and wishing he could, like so many of his companions, slip away.

The Boers had no difficulty in occupying positions from which to fire on the British as they already held Green Hill, the other side of the road and to the north-west, and Twin Peaks was vacant and swiftly manned. Also vacant, but unknown to the British, were Conical Hill to the north of Spioenkop and connected to it by a nek, and Aloe Knoll to the north-east, slightly lower than the British position, but from which a standing man could be shot. It was, however, the artillery that did the damage. From Ntabamnyama three 75mm guns and a pom-pom were brought to bear, from beyond Conical Hill another 75mm and from Twin Peaks a 75mm and a pom-pom. Behind the ridge across the top of the hill the west-facing British trench crossed a shallow depression, perfect for shelling, into which the Boers dropped their missiles, shattering rocks and filling the air with splinters. On the slight forward slope to the north-east the Conical Hill and Twin Peaks guns sprayed their fire. The British artillery was too far east to respond to the Boer batteries on Green Hill and Ntabamnyama, although it could fire on Twin Peaks. Lacking trenches, all the British could do was cling on to be killed or wounded. Woodgate was soon a victim.

The senior officers remaining were Colonel Crofton of the Royal Lancasters and Thorneycroft, and as the former was a regular he took precedence. When Warren got the news he ordered the injured

Major-general Talbot Coke, who had not led the original approach because of his incomplete recovery from a broken leg, to go up and take command. At the same time Buller, with a better view from Mount Alice, saw Thorneycroft rallying the British on the hilltop and heliographed Warren with the suggestion that the Colonel was the man to put in charge. Warren complied, but failed to tell Coke. Reinforcements were sent up, the Imperial Light Infantry and the 2nd Middlesex Regiment, the latter just in time to prevent the crumbling Lancashire Fusiliers on the right giving way; indeed, they had already done so in part and the Middlesex had to use the bayonet to restore the line.

Warren also appealed to Lyttleton for support. The 2nd Scottish Rifles and Bethune's Mounted Infantry moved forward to Spioenkop, but the 3rd King's Royal Rifle Corps were sent against Twin Peaks. They took the position, and Schalk Burger pulled back the artillery as a result. Orders to abort this attack had been ignored by the CO, Colonel Buchanan-Riddell, who was keen to avenge the defeats of the earlier Boer War, but with his death the unit withdrew and another opportunity was lost.

As the evening came on Thorneycroft could see no purpose in holding the hill. What reinforcements he had had were by now worn out, the ground was thick with dead, dying and wounded and he was himself exhausted. The command was never clearly in his

hands and the confusion had been costly. Winston Churchill had seen the situation and reported it to Warren, with a contribution of his own ideas. Warren overcame his irritation at this upstart, and sent him to see Thorneycroft to find out if reinforcement and artillery would hold the hill on the morrow, but the decision had already been taken. Down from the hill

Above **British dead on Spioenkop. The body in the foreground is a sergeant of the King's Own Lancaster Regiment.** (LSM07/3189. MFME BW6/20)

came the survivors. Down, also came the Boers, unwilling to continue the fight against such stubborn men. The stronghold of Spioenkop was to fall to the first people there the next day. Reitz was present when Botha spoke to the Boers departing in the darkness.

'*He addressed the men from the saddle, telling them of the shame that would be theirs if they deserted their posts in this hour of danger; and so eloquent was his appeal that in a few minutes the men were filing off into the dark to re-occupy their positions on either side of the Spion Kop gap…*

'*We woke with the falling of the dew … Gradually the dawn came and … then to our utter surprise we saw two men on the top triumphantly waving their hats and holding their rifles aloft… the English were gone and the hill was ours.*'

The summit, he found, was covered with dead and wounded. The artillery had done fearful slaughter. Now the task was to find survivors and get them off the hill.

On 16 October 1899 a meeting of some 100 Indians took place in Durban and were addressed by the young lawyer, Mohandas Karamchand Gandhi. He put it to them that they could not be mere spectators in the conflict and with their approval wrote to the Colonial Secretary to offer their services. While they did not know how to fight, there were other duties to be performed on the battlefield. In December Buller asked for assistance in raising an Indian Ambulance Corps and Ghandi stated the readiness of his people to work at the front. The Indian Stretcher Bearers Corps first saw service after the Battle of Colenso and was stood down but reconstituted in January 1900 and summoned to the front in anticipation of the attempt to outflank the Boers. They now provided a vital link in supporting the work of the troops bringing the wounded down to the field hospital, from which the Indian Stretcher Bearers Corps carried them to Treeves's hospital at Spearman's Farm and then from there to the railway at Frere.

Treeves wrote of the aftermath of Spioenkop:

'*The volunteer ambulance corps and the coolie bearers did excellent service. The larger number of the wounded were on the top of Spion Kop. The path down was about two miles [3.2km], was steep, and in places very difficult. The carriage of the wounded … had to be by hand… The surgeons who went after the wounded on* the top of the hill told us that the sight of the dead and injured was terrible in the extreme, the wounds having been mostly from shell and shrapnel …'

Now Buller assumed direct command himself, withdrew the troops from below Spioenkop and determined on another thrust on this front, taking the flat-topped hill of Vaalkrans, east of the second dog's ear meander, and thus opening the way to clearing the Brakfontein ridge from the east. Once more, preparations were lengthy and the Boers had time to assess the threat and counter it. Major-general A. S. Wynne, successor to Woodgate, was to attack the ridge beyond the pontoon bridge at Potgieter's Drift with the Lancashire Brigade while Lyttelton's Brigade was to throw a pontoon across the river at Munger's Drift and attack and take Vaalkrans to the north. This done,

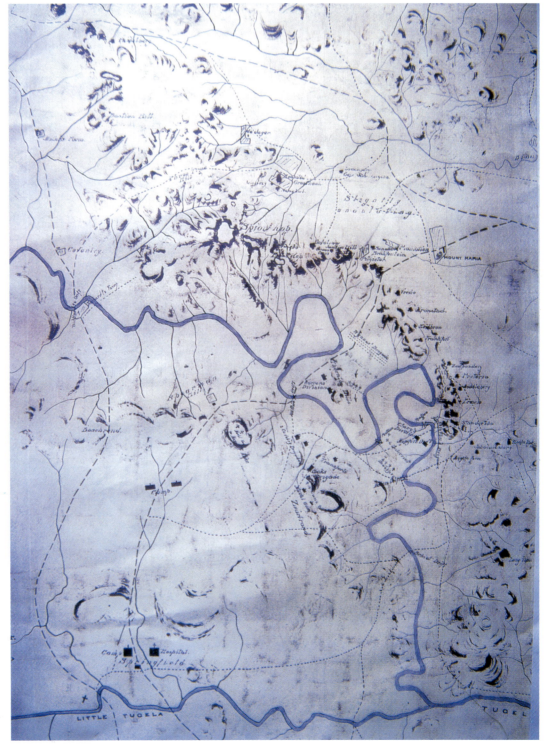

Right **Detail showing the disposition of forces at the Battle of Vaalkrans from the map of Boer positions on 5 February 1900 made by Major F. W. von Wichmann, Staats Artillerie, South African Republic. The map is not dated, but Von Wichmann refers to the Republic as 'the late' and the map was logged into the Intelligence Division, War Office, Map Room on 17 August 1903, so it is certainly not contemporary with the events it portrays. The road by Trichardt's Drift passing north of Spioenkop and the arrowhead formation of that hill can be seen.** (BL E54:11[40])

Hart's and Hildyard's Brigades were to come across under the shelter of artillery that would have been set up on Vaalkrans. They were to squeeze, somehow, between the river and the hill in order to turn westwards and take the Boers on Brakfontein Ridge in the flank.

The artillery support would consist of a 4.7in. naval gun on Mount Alice and another on Naval Gun Hill (Signal Hill) immediately to the east, to cover Wynne's attack. Two 12-pdrs. and the two newly-arrived 5in. army guns would be below Swartskop (Zwaarts Kop). The Mountain Battery, two Royal Field Artillery guns and Lieutenant Ogilvy's six 12-pdrs. would be on the top of Swartskop, but getting

them there was a challenge. The Sappers blasted the worst of the obstructive rocks away and a rough track was made. Treble oxen teams, 48 beasts, and all hands hauled the guns to the foot of the hill by night. The cable for the observation balloon was borrowed and the ascent was tackled the next night in three stages. First, the men and oxen of the previous night hauled a given gun as far up as they could. Next the escort, Scottish Fusiliers, threw their weight on the drag-ropes. The final stretch, at about 40 degrees of slope, was dealt with by men pulling on ropes that passed through blocks or pulleys either side of the top of the track to which the wire cable was fastened. By midnight two guns were up, then they rested, resuming at 4am to get the rest in place behind the sheltering trees on the northern edge of the hilltop. At 7am on that Monday, 5 February, operations began.

Wynne advanced to within a mile (1.5km) of the ridge and an artillery and rifle duel developed. Lyttleton was over the new pontoon by noon, the 1st Durham Light Infantry in the lead with 3rd King's Royal Rifles in immediate support. They had the hill by 4pm, driving off the small Boer defence and killing, according to Churchill, 'five or six armed Kaffirs'. They dug in for the counter-attack expected on the next day. The plan to place artillery on this hill was abandoned because of the rough terrain and exposure to Boer fire; dangers that appear fairly obvious from the outset and thus curious to invoke now. The Boer artillery fire was endured all Tuesday and Hildyard's Brigade relieved them that night. It became evident that the operation was stalled. Buller cabled Roberts to seek his views, given that it might cost 2,000 to 3,000 men to press on here, but Roberts contented himself with a general exhortation to relieve Ladysmith which was not constructive in the circumstances. At a conference that afternoon it was decided to withdraw and, on 8 February, the British were trailing back south of the river. The left hook had failed.

THE WESTERN FRONT

Lord Roberts and the reinforcements he was to bring were not on the scene until February 1900 and in the meantime all was not quiet. The Canadians had reached South Africa in December and now they and the Australians were engaged in an action to secure the flank of Methuen's long line of supply. Douglas, some 37 miles (60km) north-west of Belmont, was held by Boers with a forward camp at Sunnyside, about halfway between the two towns, and on the last day of 1899 a force of 100 Canadian Infantry and their machine-gun section, 250 Queensland Mounted Infantry, the Duke of Cornwall's Light Infantry and two guns of the Royal Horse Artillery under Colonel T. D. Pilcher of the Northumberland Fusiliers set out. They were fortunate in that repeated manoeuvres in

Above **C Company of the Royal Canadian Regiment storming a kopje at Sunnyside, 1 January 1900**, reads the original caption to a picture that seems somewhat posed.
(McGregor Museum, Kimberley)

recent days had ended with the British returning to Belmont, so their march caused no alarm. They reached Thornhill that evening and, shielded from detection by dust-storms, made a final approach next morning. The artillery engaged the enemy at about 11am and the Canadians, well spread out, advanced to a low ridge from which they opened fire while the Queenslanders circled left and attacked from the west. Advancing in careful rushes from cover to cover the Canadians, bayonets fixed, met the incoming Australians on the summit of Sunnyside. In the whole action only two men, the Queenslander Troopers McLeod and Jones, were killed on the British side. Trooper H. G. Hinton said of the capture of the kopje:

'I shall never forget the climbing we had without a drop of water. The sun was terribly hot. I was behind a fair-sized rock and was about to blaze away, when it occurred to me to try the Boer dodge and I put my hat on top of the rock. If my head had been as exposed as my hat I would have been with poor McLeod and Jones. My hat was not on the rock 10 seconds when a bullet went through it.'

The expedition continued to Douglas where a large stock of stores was destroyed before they withdrew to Belmont, evacuating loyalists from the town. It was a very neat operation.

On 8 February Lord Roberts and his chief of staff, Major-general Lord Horatio Herbert Kitchener, passed through Belmont on their way to the front. Altogether Roberts had brought 37,000 fresh troops to this theatre of the war. There were three new infantry divisions, the 6th under Lieutenant-general Thomas Kelly-Kenny, the 7th under Lieutenant-general C. Tucker and the 9th under Lieutenant-general Sir

Right **The Boer commanders – a group photograph taken at the conference held at Magersfontein in January 1900. Handwritten annotation on the original suggests that the man standing in the centre with a white beard is General Wessels with, to his right, Generals De la Rey, De Wet and Froneman and, on his left, Cronje.**
(NRA. MFME BW1/0)

Henry Colvile. Most significant of all was the Cavalry Division under Lieutenant-general Sir John French to which was added the mounted infantry, Hannay's Brigade and Ridley's Brigade, the City Imperial Volunteers (Mounted Infantry), Kitchener's Horse and Rimington's Scouts. Here, at last, was the promise of mobility, but it was a promise somewhat flawed. A significant proportion of the horses were unfit, having completed long sea voyages, while others were fatigued or sick from hard conditions in the previous weeks. To support this huge force, nearly 40,000 men, Kitchener reorganised the transport, previously fragmented amongst units, into a single, massive service unit with the exception of water and ammunition. It was a mistake on three counts; first it was a major administrative change made in the already sufficient confusion of a campaign, second there were not the experienced officers available to manage it, and, third, it created a tempting target for enemy irregulars.

Roberts was keen to keep Cronje guessing. The Boers held the same line south of Kimberley and it would have been preferable to head east to take Bloemfontein and then to turn north for Johannesburg and Pretoria, drawing off the besieging forces from the towns rather than resuming the direct approach that had so recently failed. But Rhodes would not be satisfied with that and issued scarcely veiled threats to surrender the town if not relieved immediately. In addition, progress in Natal was lacking, raising the possibility of a surrender of Ladysmith as well. The possibility of an advance on the Colesburg front was rejected, given the strength of the Boer presence there under De la Rey.

On 5 February the Highland Brigade and the 62nd Field Battery under General Hector MacDonald seized positions on the kopje above Koedoesberg Drift, some 16 miles (26km) west of Modder River Station. Cronje sent De Wet to oppose him, but allowed him only 350 men to do so. The action sputtered on over the next three days until, with minimal casualties, the British withdrew.

On 11 February French left his camp on the Modder River and set off south-east towards the Reit River south of Jacobsdal, giving the impression of heading for Koffiefontein some 30 miles (50km) further on. Again Cronje sent De Wet to counter the move with 450 men, a Krupp and a pom-pom which he placed near Blaauwbank, 12 miles (19km) south-east of Jacobsdal, overlooking Waterval Drift. Judging French's force too large to oppose, he gave Commandant Lubbe 100 men with whom to shadow the British and set himself to observe from concealed positions. De Wet assumed Roberts was going for Bloemfontein by way of Paardeberg with French in the van, but the British were heading north for Klip Drift on the Modder, which they secured on the

evening of 13 February. Roberts continued to feed his troops around this flank while Methuen maintained demonstrations against the Magersfontein positions. Kelly-Kenny's 6th Division was hurried up to support French on the Modder and arrived there at 1am on the 15th. The next morning the 9th and 16th Lancers led the charge of the Cavalry Division for Kimberley, more than 20 miles (35km) in the heat and dust. By 4pm they were entering the town, 124 days after the Boers had first besieged it.

Above **Map of operations on the Kimberley front from *With the Flag to Pretoria*. Major actions are marked with a cross.** (MFME BWO/30)

Still haunting the banks of the Riet, De Wet saw:

'Some provision wagons, escorted by a large convoy, were passing by, following in the wake of British troops … I … still kept in hiding with my three hundred and fifty burghers… On the following day I attacked … The three or four hundred troops who were guarding it offered a stout resistance, although they were without guns. After fighting of two hours the English received a reinforcement of cavalry, with four Armstrong guns … The battle raged until it became dark; and I think we were justified in being satisfied with what we had achieved… Our booty was enormous, and consisted of two hundred heavily-laden wagons, and eleven or twelve water carts and trollies.'

They struggled to inspan (harness) the remaining oxen and make off with their plunder. It was a serious blow to Roberts's supply arrangements and an equally serious distraction for De Wet who moved south with his gains instead of supporting Cronje.

To the north Cronje was still distracted by Methuen and by the 7th Division's attack further south at Jacobsdal. Suddenly the British were at Kimberley as well! Flight was imperative. The wagons were loaded with women and children and the whole, ponderous train of fighting men and domestic impedimenta started east. No one noticed their move in the night and it was not until the morning of 16 February that, east of Klip Drift, the trekkers were seen by Hannay's Horse. Kitchener, with Kelly-Kenny at Klip Drift, ordered pursuit and sent a message to French to head south-east from Kimberley to cut off Cronje's route to Bloemfontein. Slowed by the plodding oxen, Cronje was cut off. Although exhausted by the swoop on Kimberley and the subsequent effort to round up the besiegers, French scraped together 1,500 horsemen from the 5,000 he had started with and left at 3am on 17 February. By 10.30 the next morning he had the Boers in sight as they made to cross the Modder at Vendutie Drift and hastened to engage them, a force of some 5,000 men, with Broadwood's 2nd Brigade, the 10th Hussars, 12th Lancers and the Household Cavalry together with two batteries of the Royal Horse Artillery. And so he held them while the bulk of the army came on. It was not until evening that 6th Division made it to Paardeberg Drift, but the Boers, too slow to evade even the lumbering British, were trapped.

PAARDEBERG

With Field marshal Roberts ill at Jacobsdal, Kitchener found himself in command, somewhat uncomfortably given Kelly-Kenny's technical seniority. Nevertheless he devised a plan for the immediate attack of Cronje's laager on the morning of 18 February. His force had been augmented by the arrival of Colvile's 9th Division during the night. Kitchener intended a frontal attack on the southern bank of the Modder with pincer attacks coming in left and right along the northern banks. The area covered by this operation was some 10 miles (16km) long and four miles (6.4km) wide, centred on the laager at Vendutie Drift and extending downstream to Paardeberg Drift and upstream to Koodoosrand Drift. A shallow ring of hills defined the northern edge, from Paardeberg in

Below **The Modder River close to Vendutie Drift, looking east from the Boer Memorial, Paardeberg. The telephone poles mark the modern road, very likely the line of the road at the time.** (MFME BW14/28)

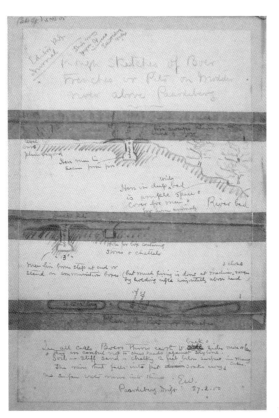

he west and Gun Hill about halfway to the laager, then the plain broadened and swept round to Koodoosrand in the east. South of the river Signal Hill was about halfway between Paardeberg and Gun Hill, Kitchener's Kopje was two miles (3.2km) due south of the laager and a series of lesser hills through Stinkfontein closed with the river to the east (see map on p. 86). The river itself cuts down into the plain to make a ravine some 20 feet (6m) deep and from five to ten times as wide. It was flowing high and fast.

The Boers dug themselves in, making deep, narrow trenches which, over the next few days, they would improve by burrowing sideways to make shelters against shrapnel. They also dug into the banks of the river to create cover for their families. The positions were well concealed. Apart from these excavations, there was little cover, so an attack would be over open ground as it neared the laager. Kelly-Kenny thought it ideal for a blockade and an artillery bombardment. Kitchener thought otherwise.

On the left Smith-Dorrien's 19th Brigade was south of the river, as was the 3rd Highland Brigade. The order came to the 19th to cross, but when he asked where, he was answered, '… Paardeberg Drift, the only one available, is unfordable; but Lord Kitchener, knowing your resourcefulness, feels sure you will get across somehow.' The Sappers got a rope across and by means of this and by linking arms, neck-deep, they struggled over to take up position on a line through Gun Hill. The 2nd King's Shropshire Light

Infantry had Gun Hill by 11am and the 1st Gordon Highlanders extended the line north-east. The Royal Canadian Regiment, under Lieutenant-colonel W. D. Otter, was told to work along the bank to link with the Shropshires. Otter had understood that, in concert with the Highlanders on the southern bank, an attack was to be made eastwards but Smith-Dorrien had not been explicit.

Hannay had made off along the southern bank to the east with four battalions of Mounted Infantry to secure Banks's and Vandenburg's Drifts, supported by the 1st Welch and 1st Essex, while the greater part of the 6th Division went straight for the south bank. By 10.30am this attack had stalled. On the north bank the Canadians had advanced as far as they could, to within some 500 yards (450m) of the Boer laager, only to come under fierce fire from the donga that runs from Gun Hill to the river.

On the east, although Hannay had established contact with French's men, a relieving force from Bloemfontein was threatening. Kitchener intervened at 11am to have the New South Wales Mounted Rifles and Kitchener's Horse hold off the Boers while the rest of the force attacked the laager from the east on both banks of the river. By 2pm this had stalled as well. In spite of mounting casualties, Kitchener pressed on, now ordering Hannay to 'gallop up and fire into the laager'. It was a murderous order. Hannay obeyed, and is buried where he fell.

The Canadians had been lying on the Veldt most of the day under a relentless sun. The Boer marksmanship was good as ever and the slightest movement had brought down fire. Now Kitchener ordered Colvile's three and a half companies of the 2nd Duke of Cornwall's Light Infantry under Lieutenant-colonel W. Aldworth to carry the laager by storm. At 4pm Aldworth came to Otter and told him what he was about to do. At 5.15 the bugles sounded the charge and many Canadians, tired of baking in the sun, joined in. Smith-Dorrien, from the eminence of Gun Hill, was amazed. 'It was quite irregular,' he said later, 'that my troops have been ordered to execute such an important movement, except through me, as any possibility of my supporting the charge … was effectually prevented …' Aldworth lay dead with many of his men and of the Canadians. It was an entirely avoidable disaster.

De Wet and his men reached the area at about 4.30pm south of the buildings and kraals of Stinkfontein.

'What a spectacle we saw! All round the laager were the guns of the English, belching forth death and destruction, while from within it at every moment, as each successive shell tore up the ground, there rose a cloud - a dark red cloud of dust.'

He conferred with General Botha, who, it was decided, would go for Stinkfontein while De Wet

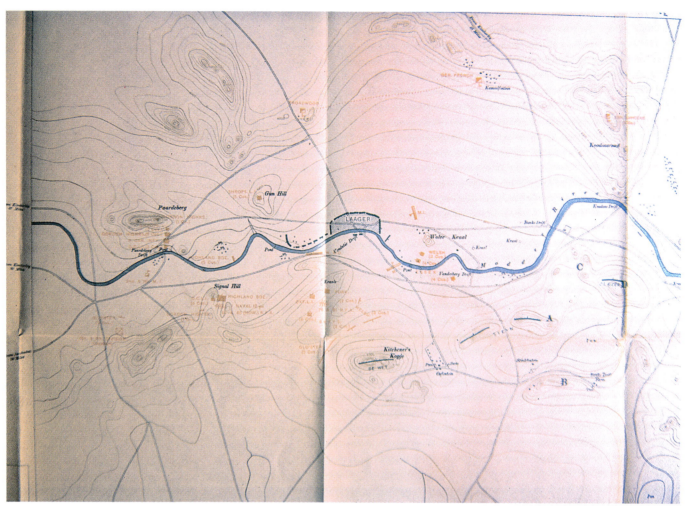

Above **Situation map of Paardeberg, night of 18 to 19 February 1900, from Maurice** *History of the War.* (LSM. MFME BW6/33)

Right **The memorial to Colonel Hannay, looking west towards Paardeberg, which has a telecommunications tower on the top.** (MFME BW14/34)

went for the high ground. The *uitlanders* of Kitchener's Horse were swept off Kitchener's Kopje or forced to surrender. The 75mm Krupp and the Maxim-Nordenfeldt pom-pom were installed in stone-built emplacements constructed during the night and they were ready not merely to resist attack, but to dominate the southern sector of the battlefield and the escape route for Cronje.

'By daybreak the English had crept up to within a short distance of our lines. It was the Krupp and the Maxim-Nordenfeldt that gave our answer. But we had to be very sparing of our ammunition, for it was almost exhausted, and it would take at least five days to get a fresh supply from Bloemfontein.'

Meanwhile the shells continued to fall on Cronje's laager. The wagons were smashed and the animals killed. It would have been possible for fighting men to have escaped, provided they abandoned their goods and families, and a few did. The majority stayed, demoralised and unable to hit back at their tormentors. Lord Roberts arrived to assume command and was himself depressed by what he saw. British casualties had been severe, 320 dead and 942 wounded, and he actually contemplated withdrawing

to Klip Drift before Boer reinforcements arrived. Some small gains against De Wet were made by the 2nd Gloucestershire Regiment on 19 and 20 February, but he still held the kopje. The issue was settled by De Wet's lack of supplies. The last of his artillery rounds was fired and the guns were spirited away. As French's men joined in the attack, the men of De Wet's force were threatened with being surrounded.

'In all haste I ordered my men to retire... All made good their retreat, with the exception of Veldt-Cornet Speller, of Wepener, who, to my great regret, was taken prisoner with fourteen men ... the English had very speedily taken up positions to the right and left, with guns and maxims, and for a good nine miles of our retreat we were under their fire.'

The laager was now totally surrounded once more. The bombardment continued. On 23 February it began to rain, flooding the trenches and filling the dug-outs. On 26 February the demand to surrender was again refused; it was the eve of the anniversary of Majuba, the great Boer victory of the first Boer War. The Canadians relieved the Cornwalls in the trenches on the west of the enclave. Smith-Dorrien's 19th Brigade had been reinforced by the Argyll and Sutherland Highlanders and by two companies of the Black Watch, as well as by a company of Royal Engineers. It was clear that, if the Boer line could be taken beyond the donga, the laager would be vulnerable to direct rifle fire and untenable.

At 2.15am on 27 February six companies of the Royal Canadian Regiment advanced in silence, in two lines, with the Sappers in the second line. If detected, the second line would entrench. Suddenly there was a rattle of tin cans on wire - an alarm! The night was sparking with rifle flashes, the Canadians went to ground returning fire and the Sappers dug. Someone gave an order to retire, or so it seemed. Two-thirds of the Canadians crawled or ran back, but the rest held on and as the day dawned looked down on the laager. Then a white flag appeared, and another. So many Boers appeared out of the ground that, Smith-Dorrien remarked, it was like the resurrection. Cronje surrendered to Roberts and with him 4,105 Boers. A. B. 'Banjo' Paterson, the Australian poet and writer, described the defeated general as

'a square cut farmer-like man with dark eyebrows and a short beard, dressed in the outer costume of a long black frock coat, light trousers, tan boots and a slouch hat.'

and of the Boers themselves he said 'They were as brave a set of men as ever born.'

In spite of their courage the British had, at last, a victory over their adversaries in person.

BULLER'S RIGHT HOOK

After the retreat from the Spioenkop and Vaalkrans front to Chieveley, Buller immediately undertook a renewed and closer study of the terrain north of Colenso. On his side of the river, east of the town, were hills held by the Boers, Nhlangwini immediately

Below **Boer trenches crowned the heights of the hills along the Tugela.** (LSM07/3541. MFME BW6/3)

Left **Ambulance wagons cross the Tugela by a pontoon bridge built by the Royal Engineers.** (McM. MFME BW10/16)

Below **British troops resting on a hill captured from the Boers during the successful break-through, according to the contemporary caption. The location is uncertain.** (LSM07/967. MFME BW6/7)

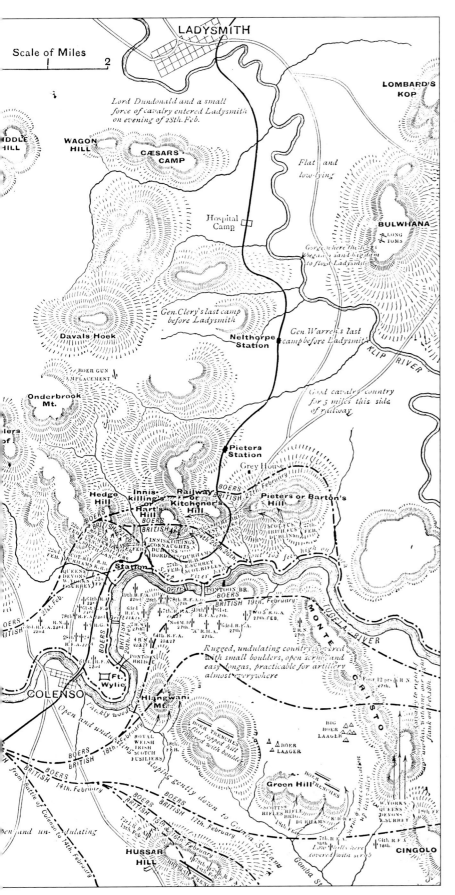

Scale of Miles

to the north-east, Cingolo six miles (9.6km) to the east, beyond Green Hill, and, in a semi-circle based on that axis, east to west, Monte Christo, Clump Hill and Fuzzy Hill with lesser hills between. North of the river, beyond the blown railway bridge over Onderbroekspruit, close to its junction with the Tugela, were a succession of hills around which the railway wound on the way to Pieters and Ladysmith. Full frontal attack had been proven too costly and a new approach was needed. Buller had few cavalry, but experienced infantry and, at last, real strength in artillery. The advance was now to be an accumulation of smaller, limited advances, allowing the artillery to be brought up before the next step was attempted. The artillery was to fire on specific targets as much as possible, trenches and gun emplacements, rather than unleash a general bombardment. Buller began with Hussar Hill, south-east of Colenso, on 16 February.

The pace was deliberate. The heat was intense and all water had to be brought up from Frere in 200 gallon tanks, just enough to fill the water-bottles of the men of a single battalion. Buller, as ever, was mindful of the welfare of his troops. Hussar Hill fell to Dundonald and Barton's Brigade and the former moved on at once towards Cingolo. This came within an ace of disaster when, the next day, Dundonald's men nearly found themselves fighting Hildyard's who were coming up the other side. On the right the advance flowed over Monte Christo on 18 and 19 February and Colonel C. H. Norcott's (formerly Lyttleton's) Brigade advanced to the east of Nhlangwini. Outflanked, the Boers on this vital feature drifted away and Barton's occupied it the next day with insignificant resistance. The southern bank was Buller's.

The Boers could be seen retreating on the other side, pulling back into the hills. The news from Lord Roberts was that Free Staters were returning from Natal to his front, so hopes rose of the opposition on the Tugela heights being little more than a rearguard. Two days passed while the next line of attack was considered in the light of the information provided by Lieutenant-colonel A. E. Sandbach, the senior intelligence officer. The first task was actually to cross the river, something that appeared too difficult to do on the west to east section that passed immediately north of Monte Christo, given the depth of the banks,

Left A map from *With the Flag to Pretoria*, showing Buller's operations for the relief of Ladysmith. The modern road passes west and north of Hart's Hill and the present railway passes through a tunnel in the north-western slope of Hart's Hill. Part of the old railbed forms a spur line to a quarry in the western side of the hill and the old road survives in part, accessible from the point at which the railway and new road meet north of Railway Hill.

Above **British graves near Onderbroekspruit, under Wynne's (or Hedge) Hills, Colenso.** (MFME BW15/12)

Main picture **Colenso cooling towers from Hart's Hill. The new railway is on the extreme right with the old road below. On the left the Nhlangwini ridge stretches south. In the foreground is the modern quarry.** (MFME BW15/18)

Above **From the old railway embankment south of the Irish Fusiliers Memorial, looking south-west, the new bridge carrying the railway over Onderbroekspruit can be seen.** (MFME BW15/33)

Above **The memorial to the Irish Fusiliers, seen from beside the modern railway line, stands just north-east of the confluence of Langverwagspruit and the Tugela, alongside the remaining abutments of Pom-Pom Bridge. As comparison with contemporary pictures shows (see p. 92), the trees and scrub disguise the landscape fought over a hundred years ago.** (MFME BW15/15)

Above **Boer positions on the top of Hart's Hill. The ground is level for some 150 yards (135m) in front of this trench, giving an excellent killing field. There is a sangar or possibly a gun emplacement on the little summit above.** (MFME BW15/19)

along the railway, the old one, to take position above the Tugela ready to assault the hill.

Darkness fell with the ground before the Boer trenches on the summit of the hill strewn with dead and wounded. Those who were to live to tell the tale would wait two days for succour. The next day the hillside was striped with brown lines, sheltering troops who clung on behind stone walls, exchanging fire with the Boers through the day. Buller learned of the plight of the untended wounded on the evening of 24 February and a truce was arranged for the following morning.

British casualties in these operations now amounted to some 1,200 men killed and wounded. Merely to pass on to the next hill was to invite the same slaughter. But now a new opportunity was offered. A site had been located for the pontoon further downstream, between Hart's Hill Falls and the rapids, while the steep northern bank provided cover from view and fire by the Boers on, from west to east, Hart's, Railway and Pieters Hills. The Sappers moved the pontoon after nightfall on 26 February and it was ready by 10am the next day. Over it went units now mixed as those facing the Boers westwards remained in place, so here Barton's 6th Brigade had acquired the Dublins from the 5th and started for Pieters. Railway Hill was the objective of Lieutenant-colonel Walter Kitchener's (formerly the wounded Wynne's) Lancashires plus the 2nd West Yorkshires and Norcott's was to finish the job at Hart's Hill. The artillery was massed south of the river on Monte Christo and other heights. The whole strength of the British was to be visited upon the Boers.

Deneys Reitz was riding to join his commando, which had gone to reinforce the men on Pieters, as the guns spoke.

'... a bombardment ... broke out ahead of us, and, when we came to the rear of Pieters Heights, we saw the ridge ... going up in smoke and flame.'

Pieters is actually a high, hilly ridge running north and south, today crossed by the road coming south from the little town of that name, and it was up the southern slope the Irish Fusiliers were now climbing, hit by fire from Railway Hill but racing on to displace the Heidelberg Commando. The Scots Fusiliers moved forward, covered by the Irish, but now ran into tough resistance as they strove for the next hillock. By 2.30pm they had it. Reitz saw it.

'... we caught the fierce rattle of Mauser rifles followed by British infantry swarming over the skyline, their bayonets flashing in the sun. Shouts and cries reached us, and we could see men desperately thrusting and clubbing. Then a rout of burghers broke back from the hill ... We went too ...'

Down to the left of the Irish, in the valley, the West Yorkshires had worked up alongside Railway Hill and from there, with the South Lancashires and,

virtually a gorge, so the first objective chosen was on the left, the formation of hills just north of the little kopjes that was to become known as Wynne Hills. At the time only a single hill was thought to be there, a second one covered with Boers was unsuspected. A pontoon bridge was secured across the Tugela at Studam, a mile (1.6km) north-east of Colenso station on the south to north reach of the river. On the afternoon of 22 February Wynne managed, in a bloody encounter, to secure the position but it was still overlooked by the Boers to the west.

On the east of Langverwagspruit, which flows into the Tugela under what was Pom-Pom Bridge, and south of the mouth of the modern railway tunnel, loomed the next hill, now known as Hart's or Inniskilling Hill. The next afternoon Hart led his Irish Brigade, supported by half of Norcott's Brigade,

further left, the King's Own went for Railway Hill. The East Surreys were pushing up Hart's Hill, supported on their left by 1st Rifle Brigade. Soon all but the final peak of Pieters were in British hands and a last rush by the Irish Fusiliers rendered that untenable to the Boers. The Irish Guards were formed in recognition of Queen Victoria's 'brave Irish soldiers'.

There was no general pursuit; Buller's men were in no condition to undertake it. At about 6pm riders were seen approaching Ladysmith and some Natal Carbineers rode out to investigate. They found men of their own regiment from Major Hubert Gough's Composite Regiment. With the Natal Carbineers and

the Imperial Light Horse riding abreast to share the honour, Buller's men entered Ladysmith. The first need was to get supplies into the town, not to go chasing Boers.

Nurse Kate Driver came on a man peering against the sun late that afternoon.

'I asked him what he was staring at. "Look," he said. He was seeing men on horseback riding over the ridge towards Caesar's Camp… "Why don't you report to the gunners that the enemy are upon us?" He said very quietly, "They might be our own men"… As the column reached Caesar's Camp we heard a sudden shout, and then a burst of shouting from the soldiers stationed there, the dear, valiant, starving Manchesters. Oh, then we knew! This really was the much-longed-for Relief Force!'

THE ROAD TO BLOEMFONTEIN

After the fall of Paardeberg and with the capital of the Orange Free State now directly threatened, De la Rey withdrew from Colesburg and came back to oppose Roberts's advance. President Steyn appointed De Wet as his C-in-C and positions were taken up at Poplar Grove, some 10 miles (16km) east of Paardeberg. On 7 March President Kruger arrived to pay the troops a visit, just as Roberts was resuming his march eastwards. De Wet wrote:

Left **Buller's troops make their formal entry into Ladysmith, 2 March 1900.** (McM. MFME BW11/17)

Below **British troops advance on Poplar Grove.** (McG. MMKP8534)

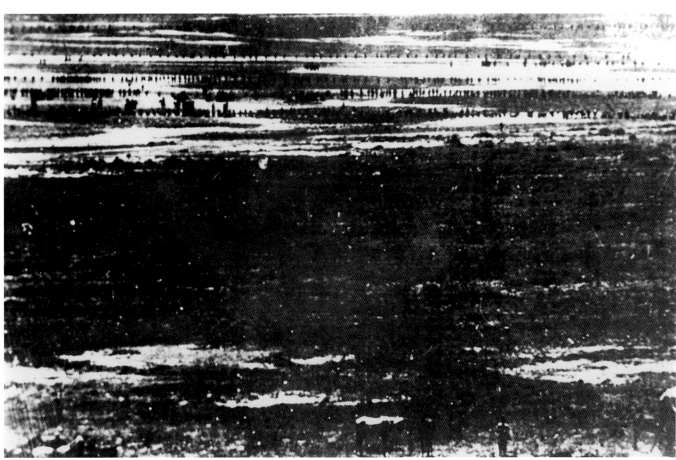

'Hardly had the harness been taken off the tired animals when a telegram arrived, saying that Petrusburg was already in the hands of the English. President Kruger was thus compelled to return without a moment's delay. I … rode to the positions where my burghers were stationed.

'Again I was confronted with the baleful influence of Cronje's surrender. A panic had seized my men. Before the English had even got near enough to shell our positions … the wild flight began… It was a flight such as I had never seen before, and shall never see again… In the evening we came to Abraham's Kraal … some eighteen miles from Poplar Grove.'

Had the British moved faster, De Wet observed, they could have surrounded the remaining army, but

even after a week's rest the horses were tired. The fight at Abraham's Kraal was a different matter. A kopje stands close by the south bank of the Modder west of the confluence with Kaalspruit and the hills of Driefontein rise from the Veldt some five miles (8km) to the south. Here De Wet had managed to persuade some of his men to stand together with the Johannesburg and Pretoria Police under Philip Botha and a small French contingent with which Olivier d'Etchegayen was serving. He described the dispositions.

'Our right, with the Modder River beyond, consisted of about 400 men of the Johannesburg Politie, with a Krupp gun, an Armstrong, and two Maxims. Then a space in the plain, where a commando of 200 men, with three cannon and a Maxim gun, constituting our centre, had taken up position early in the morning. Finally, to our south, on our left, 300 men on a round kopje, fairly high.'

Of the quality of the Boers d'Etchegayen remarked:

'Easily depressed and as easily elated, without any apparent cause, they are a curious jumble of virtues and failings … The sort of panics frequent among them are due, I think, rather to their total lack of organization than to their temperament; for, not to speak of individual instances of valour, by no means rare among them, the Johannesburg Politie, with their very primitive discipline, have shown what might have been done by the Boers with some slight instruction and some slight discipline.'

Against these positions the British moved on the morning of 10 March. The fighting lasted all day with little change in the positions occupied by either side. French, leading the southernmost column, attempted to outflank De la Rey, but the Boers were able to contain the movement, while on the northern end of the front the police held against the fiercest assaults. But, as De Wet reported,

'… with the setting of the sun a change came over them. Once more panic seized them; leaving their positions, they retreated in haste towards Bloemfontein. And now they were only a disorderly crowd of terrified men blindly flying before the enemy.'

To be fair, the police had only forsaken their positions when the 1st Essex Regiment had come in so hard that the horse lines, and thus their means of movement, were threatened.

The way to Bloemfontein now lay open before Roberts, at the cost of 82 dead that day, and 344 wounded. Once more De Wet attempted to rally his men, and once more he failed. Roberts pressed on, his men on half rations and his animals collapsing in increasing numbers. On 13 March they entered the capital of the Orange Free State unopposed.

Trooper N. T. Seccombe of the Queensland Mounted Infantry wrote of that time:

'Advancing at the rate of about 10 miles [16km] a day, we were cut down to half rations, three biscuits a day – very hard – half a pound of tinned beef and one quart of tea… The poor wretches, horses and mules, that die by the wayside would soften the heart of the hardest.'

And Trooper Samuel Ball, New South Wales Mounted Rifles said:

'It is quite a usual thing to see dead horses here. At present there are more than 300 carcases in one heap, besides others scattered over the farm… There are now 1,200 sick horses on this farm and on average half a dozen die daily.'

The horses were not the only ones unwell. Seccombe remarked:

'I had one day's sickness at Paardeberg from drinking impure water and thought I was going to die. A large number of us were in the same plight.'

THE CHIMERA OF VICTORY

With Kimberley and Ladysmith relieved, it seemed that all that was necessary was to proceed to Johannesburg and Pretoria, relieving Mafeking as a side-show, and accept the surrender of the Boers. The Boers, however, had a different view. From a war with clear-cut objectives - this ridge, that town, this territory - the conflict steadily altered into one for control of people, people who might stick like mud or flow like water. To win such a fight new techniques would be needed, much had to be learnt; much would not be learnt at this time, and many mistakes would be made. The purpose of the British was to force the Boers to surrender their sovereignty and it would have been easier to do if the purpose of the Boers had been equally clear. The Boers lacked any positive objective; they simply did not want to give up. It was, by now, entirely obvious that they could not win the war but they were, at this stage, almost unanimous in refusing to surrender. The cost to their people was to be immense.

The British paused at Bloemfontein and Kimberley to rest and the Boers did much the same. De Wet gave his men leave to go home until 25 March, aware that many would not return to fight, but happier to lead willing, rather than reluctant, men. Roberts expected Boers to surrender and on 15 March offered generous terms – if they surrendered their rifles, took an oath of allegiance and returned to their homes they would be granted amnesty. So they handed in the oldest weapon they could obtain and went off to hide the Mauser for use another day. The Boer forces still in the field included General Steenkamp's commando at Prieska in the north-west Cape, Snyman at Mafeking, Du Toit north of Kimberley, De Wet and De la Rey north of Bloemfontein, Olivier north-east of Colesberg, Prinsloo guarding the approaches from Natal to the Free State and Botha's Transvaalers north of Ladysmith on the Biggarsburg range. When intelligence was received of Olivier's move northwards the response was too little and too late. The Boer general evaded the force under General French sent to block his passage at Thaba Nchu, the 'Place of Waters', 40 miles (60km) east of Bloemfontein.

Roberts was taking his time. Buller has been regarded as the great procrastinator of the war, but failures of transport and dependence on the single, slender rail line slowed Roberts just as surely as the need to rebuild the railway north of the Tugela delayed progress in Natal. Indeed, the Commander-in-Chief telegraphed Buller three days after the relief of Ladysmith to state that it was not wise to start extensive operations in Natal and that operations against the Drakensberg passes would be very hazardous. But most important of all in Ladysmith was the presence of disease, enteric, or typhoid, fever. Ten people a day had been dying of it at the end of the siege, and good diet and sanitation were needed to prevent it. Now the troops in Bloemfontein started to go down with enteric, the result of drinking polluted water and of woefully poor sanitation. Buller might fuss over the welfare of his men to, some thought, the detriment of military operations, but the neglect of Roberts and Kitchener was quite as detrimental.

The new character of the war was already starting to show itself. The Dutch of the far north of Cape Colony had risen and, as the British made their way into the Free State, they had also to move in the opposite direction to put down the rebellion. Brigadier Sir Herbert Settle led a column from Orange River due west to Prieska while Colonel Sir Charles Parsons took another west from Victoria West to Carnarvon, the two eventually to meet at Kenhardt. On 14 March Parson's force, the 2nd Canadian Mounted Rifles, some Western Australian Mounted Infantry, Derbyshire Yeomanry and New Zealand Mounted Infantry, set off across the Karroo in a column several miles long. They plodded the 80 miles (130km) to Carnarvon, rested and, on 21 March, moved on towards Van Wyksvlei. Lieutenant E. W. B. Morrison, Royal Canadian Field Artillery, wrote of the plight of the horses.

'… we will come upon a horse of the advanced guard standing by the roadside, swaying groggily on its legs, its neck stretched out and its eyes glazing in death. When it hears the clank of the guns and the trampling of the horses in the column it will reel forward in a game effort to join the ranks, only to tumble in a heap. The battery passes on and a minute later the sharp crack of a pistol …'

It took two days to reach the next town, where three rebels were captured. Then heavy rain broke a two-year drought and the roads turned to slippery

Left **Enteric fever was not the only sickness encountered. This photo from Lieutenant Barton's journal was taken while he was in Partland Hospital, Rondebosch with 'sun fever'.** (NRA. MFME BW17/22)

skid-pans. They were stuck there for five days, bored, with stomach troubles and reprimanded for getting drunk. Two men died and lie buried on the Karroo. Driver Robert Bradley drowned while watering horses and a New Zealander, Private T. H. Hempton, died of enteric. By the end of March there were 50 sick here and 24 back at Carnarvon. On 4 April they were ordered back to De Aar and 611 troops, 118 black drivers, 10 guns, 57 supply wagons, 559 horses, 571 mules, 96 donkeys and 32 oxen left Van Wyksvlei. A week later they reported back to base. Apart from showing the flag amongst a populace of doubtful loyalty, little had been achieved, and much of the activity for the rest of the war would, for the majority involved, be as tedious and apparently useless.

Settle's column had a very similar experience, though one incident brightened the tale. Sam Hughes, who had been disappointed by his exclusion from the organisation of the Canadian force for South Africa, managed to persuade Settle that he was, as a Colonial, a fine scout. Thus Lieutenant-colonel S. Hughes, Royal Canadian Rifles, found himself in the vanguard. In the same rains that had confined Parson's force to Van Wyksvlei Hughes was sent with six men to reconnoitre the town of Upington, 90 miles (150km) north-west of Prieska. After two days' ride they arrived in as much dust and with as much noise as they could raise; the rebels fled. Hughes took up a defensive position and waited nervously. Eight scouting Dutchmen were captured, but Sam was still in place

when the main column arrived three days later. It was an arrogant and successful bluff.

When he assumed command Lord Roberts also required a Chief of Scouts. The American Indian fighter and scout Frederick Russell Burnham was busy at the time in his house in Scagway, Alaska, preparing to prospect for gold, when a telegram came: 'Lord Roberts appoints you on his personal staff … If you accept, come at once quickest way possible.' Burnham had arrived in time to see the relief of Kimberley and attempt a reconnaissance of the laager at Paardeberg by floating down the Modder River under a box at night. At 4pm on 30 March Major Burham was ordered to scout the country between Bloemfontein and Thaba Nchu and report his observations to Brigadier-general R. G. Broadwood who was withdrawing westwards with 1,700 men, 2nd Cavalry Brigade, Lieutenant-colonel Edwin Alderson's Mounted Infantry Brigade and Q and U Batteries, Royal Horse Artillery. There were also a number of civilian refugees. Not only was Broadwood aware of Olivier's presence to the east in superior numbers, but also Burnham had wind of De Wet's being somewhere around.

SANNASPOS

De Wet was, indeed, on that road, intending to destroy the Bloemfontein waterworks near Sannaspos (Sanna's Post) and thus exacerbate the typhoid crisis in the town. Broadwood had bivouacked that night close to the waterworks and east of the Modder River, while in the other direction General Colvile was settled at

Main picture **From the Sannaspos visitors' viewpoint, looking east, the modern road strikes away like an arrow. To the right of it, marked with white posts, the old road leads to the railway station while the bushes alongside Koorn Spruit go to the right towards the rail bridge over the stream.** (MFME BW12/28)

Right **British graves at Sannaspos. They are near the station in which there is a small museum.** (MFME BW 12/25)

Bushman's Kop, ten miles (16km) away, from which messages were relayed on to Bloemfontein. De Wet took 350 men to Koorn Spruit which runs north just to the west of Sannaspos and the rest of his force, under Cronje, Wessels, Froneman and Piet De Wet, some 1,150 men, took up postions east of the Modder River on ridges overlooking Sannaspos, with their four or five guns, ready to open fire at daybreak on 31 March.

Burnham was running late and took to the road that night, reaching farm buildings overlooking Koorn Spruit at about 3am. Approaching with caution he detected the Boers at the drift and moved north to find a way round. At this moment De Wet was as ignorant of Broadwood's presence as anyone – his intention was still to attack the waterworks. As dawn broke,, Burnham heard artillery fire and, standing, saw Broadwood's wagons leaving the waterworks towards the drift on Koorn Spruit.

'The morning light penetrating the dark shadows of the spruit right in front of me showed it full of Boer horsemen - hundreds of them. They had dismounted and lined the bank of the spruit ... now I realized that this was an ambush on a large scale ... I drew from my pocket a large red silk handkerchief, about two feet [60cm] square, that I always carried for signalling. Sitting on my horse, I waved this frantically for about ten

Left **The road west from Sannaspos towards Koorn Spruit, which cannot readily be identified, and the ridge on which, next to the modern road, the Boer Memorial and viewpoint stands.** (MFME BW12/27)

Right **The waterworks Sannaspos (Sannas Post) from which Bloemfontein was supplied.** (RE23/85. MFME BW18/14)

Below **A group photograph taken of men returning from South Africa on SS *Dunottar Castle* in late 1900. Major Burnham, who had been seriously wounded during the advance to Komati Poort east of Pretoria, is standing third from left and the journalist Winston Churchill is seated second from right.** (MFME BW17/13)

minutes, but there was not a single British scout to observe my warning, and no advance guard appeared in front of the oncoming transport wagons.'

Burnham was seen, but by the Boers, who took him prisoner, and from a stone kraal at the farmhouse he watched. Broadwood's force was fighting a rearguard action against the Boers east of the Modder while he fell back to cross Koorn Spruit. David Plant, from Victoria, Australia, had enlisted in Roberts's Horse and had been given the order to saddle up and move out for Bloemfontein. He recalled:

'Some of the men were eating breakfast consisting of a piece of bread as they rode, some were filling their pipes and others yarning… A heavy shell fire continued behind us, when all of a sudden we saw the wagons forming into a laager, so we thought the Boers must be in front of us.'

As each wagon descended into the spruit the guard and driver were captured and the wagon turned left or right along the bed of the stream in an orderly and efficient way. De Wet recalled:

'The carts were filled with English from ThabaNchu. I was very glad that the women and children should thus reach a place of safety, before the firing began… very shortly the soldiers began to pour into the drift in the greatest disorder. As soon as they reached the stream they were met by the cry of "Hands up!"'

Soon some 200 had been disarmed. Finally the British smelled a rat, probably because no one could be seen emerging from the drift on the western side and climbing the ridge and the column was starting to tail back from the spruit. The Horse Artillery turned, the troops turned and all made their way back under a gale of Mauser fire, taking cover behind the railway station. Wagons and oxen milled about in confusion, their African drivers killed or fleeing. In an attempt to cover this retreat Major Edward Phipps-Hornby, in command of Q Battery, brought his guns into action

so close to the well-positioned Boers that they could not last long, but at least they made some reply to the Mauser fire. The guns were eventually recovered by hand, men braving the rifle fire to haul guns and limbers to the shelter of the station buildings. Meanwhile the Boers east of the Modder were seeking a crossing on the British flank and, fortunately, failing to find one. The pressure of Broadwood's many men, aided by the covering fire of the artillery, was so great that they flowed left and right of De Wet's small force, crossing the spruit above and below, with four guns of Q Battery. The 3rd Mounted Infantry and Roberts's Horse covered their departure, with the New Zealanders the last to quit the field. By 4pm, Burnham recalls, De Wet's column was 13 miles (21km) away to the north-east with 428 prisoners, seven guns and 117 wagons. A notable success.

REDDERSBURG

Taking only a few companions, De Wet now made a reconnaissance sweep to the south and soon became aware of a small British force falling back from Dewetsdorp to Reddersburg. This comprised three

Above **Attempts were made to solve the problems of animal haulage by employing traction engines powered by steam. Although they could pull many times the weight, they were prey to bogging down in wet weather or in drifts and had difficulty on rough terrain.** (McM. MFME BW12/9)

companies of the Royal Irish Rifles and two companies of Mounted Infantry of Gatacre's Division, under one Captain McWhinnie. McWhinnie had reported to Gatacre and had received orders to retire, but he got no support.

On 1 April De Wet had refreshed his strength, now standing at 110, with men who rejoined after having surrendered to the British, and had also sent north for reinforcements. Those who had rejoined were either unarmed or without adequate ammunition. They shadowed the British and when, on the evening of 2 April, the soldiers camped on one side of a hill, the Boers were on the other. Messages to General Froneman, who had left Sannaspos the day before, bringing men and three guns, stung him into renewed efforts in his forced march but, as the British pressed on during the morning of 3 April, they saw the dust of the Boer column. Immediately, at Mostertshoek, they occupied a ridge north of the road. The Boers took position on the neighbouring kopjes and their guns were there by late afternoon. The British passed a cold night, surrounded and with their

only hope a relief column from Gatacre. At dawn on 4 April the shelling began again. There were, by now, British troops to the west, in a position to intervene. De Wet wrote:

'I have never been able to understand why the great force, stationed at Reddersberg, made no attempt to come … they never stirred a foot to come and help their comrades. And it was fortunate for us … we should have stood no chance at all …

'To oppose successfully such bodies of men as our burghers had to meet during this war demanded rapidity of action more than anything else. We had to be quick at fighting, quick at reconnoitring, quick (if it became necessary) at flying!'

At 11am the British showed the white flag. De Wet took, he said, 470 prisoners. There were a dozen dead and three dozen or so wounded on the British side, one dead and six wounded on the Boer. General Gatacre was sacked and sent home.

Now De Wet broke his own rules by getting drawn into a static fight. He learned that 1,600 men of Brabant's Horse and the Cape Mounted Rifles under

Colonel E. H. Dalgety had taken up a position to defend the crossing of the Caledon River just outside Wepener at Jammerbergdrif (Tammersbergsdrift) on the Dewetsdorp road. These units were raised from loyalist colonials, many of them Afrikaners regarded by De Wet as mercenary traitors to the Boer cause. He could not resist making the attempt to capture them. The first contact was on 7 April and the British were surrounded on the 9th. Classic siege operations ensued, with the Boers attempting night attacks and saps while the defenders held them at bay with rifle and artillery fire. The approach of two substantial British columns from Bloemfontein and from Reddersberg caused De Wet to break off the siege and make for ThabaNchu, having lost five killed and 13 wounded against British casualties of 33 killed and 132 wounded during the 16-day siege. The attempt to capture the Boers as they retreated was an entire failure, in spite of Ian Hamilton's mounted infantry repossessing the territory east of Bloemfontein, including the waterworks, Pole-Carew's 11th Division holding the Dewetsdorp road and French operating to the east. The gaps were still too big and the Boers leaked away northwards. They had caused a good deal of trouble, but the waterworks had been regained and the railway's operation was never compromised.

Near Boshof, north-east of Kimberley, the European Legion under Comte Villebois-Mareuil, now a general, attempted to show the Boers how to fight. Thinking that only 200 to 300 men held Boshof, they pushed boldly forward to a ridge about 6 miles (10km) east of the town. Methuen had, unknown to Villebois, just arrived and on 5 April some 750 men of the Imperial Yeomanry and the Kimberley Mounted Corps with 4th Field Artillery caught the Europeans there. The French general was killed and the Russian Prince Nikolai Bagration-Mukhransky was wounded and captured. On the British side Sergeant Patrick Campbell, the estranged husband of the famous actress, lost his life. A wild olive tree is said to mark the place at which General Villebois-Mareuil died.

THE GREAT ADVANCE

At the beginning of May the British were ready to move forward once again. To the west Lieutenant-general Sir Archibald Hunter, with his new 10th Division, made up of Hart's and Barton's Brigades from Natal, joined Methuen's 1st at Kimberley. At Ladysmith Buller had three divisions and three mounted brigades. In the centre, to advance on the axis of the railway from Bloemfontein, Roberts had French's Cavalry Division on the left, Ian Hamilton's force with two infantry, one mounted infantry and one cavalry brigade on the right, and, between them, the 7th and 11th Divisions. Kelly-Kenny's 6th provided the Bloemfontein garrison with the 3rd

Division to the south and further forces to follow up the advance. On 3 May they moved forward.

Roberts's route took him over a succession of rivers, each a barrier defended by the Boers and each a line they were soon forced to abandon as they were outflanked by the British mounted troops and battered by the artillery. At the Vet River the Australians and New Zealanders went to take Coetzee Drift, six miles (10km) west of the blown railway crossing. Lieutenant Samuel Harris, 2nd Western Australian Mounted Infantry, was sent forward to locate the river crossing, having, like everyone else in his unit, volunteered for the job. Having found the place, he reported back and the attack went in. Then, as they went forward,

'... we were greeted by a perfect hail of bullets. Down we went... We replied with volley after volley ... after about quarter of an hour ... their fire ceased somewhat. We then advanced by rushes from the right, until our right flank was in line with the farmhouse that was flying the white flag. They opened up a hellish fire from this building, and being at close range it took effect.

'We then received the order to put in three volleys of magazine fire, fix bayonets and charge, which we did. When we got onto the kopje their fire ceased... we were relieved by the Grenadier Guards ... Next morning I am pleased to say, the house from which we were fired at was blown up with all its contents.'

French's attempts both to outflank and to surround Boer forces were futile. Banjo Paterson explained:

'... in the open country a column could be seen 10 miles off, and there is no doubt that if French had moved a day earlier, the Boers would have moved a day earlier. There is no longer any credit for driving the Boers from a position. We have so many men that while we attack in front, we can send an overwhelming force to the rear, so they have to go. The thing is to catch up with them. The horses are so fagged they cannot raise a charge at the end of a long day.'

The British had greater problems with their transport and supplies than with the enemy. Lieutenant Leslie O. Wilson, RMLI was with the naval 4.7in. guns wrote about the solution his unit found to the transport problem.

'We were also most fortunate with respect to our baggage. As our ammunition was of such enormous weight ... not more than forty rounds could be carried in one bullock wagon, consequently when we had fired off forty rounds we had a spare wagon ... By putting ammunition on every wagon, we were able to say, with truth, that all our wagons were "ammunition wagons", and ... they were never separated from us and put in the baggage train.'

This arrangement led to real trouble when a staff officer found all sorts of personal kit, tents, cooking utentsils and so on in the wagons. The matter went as

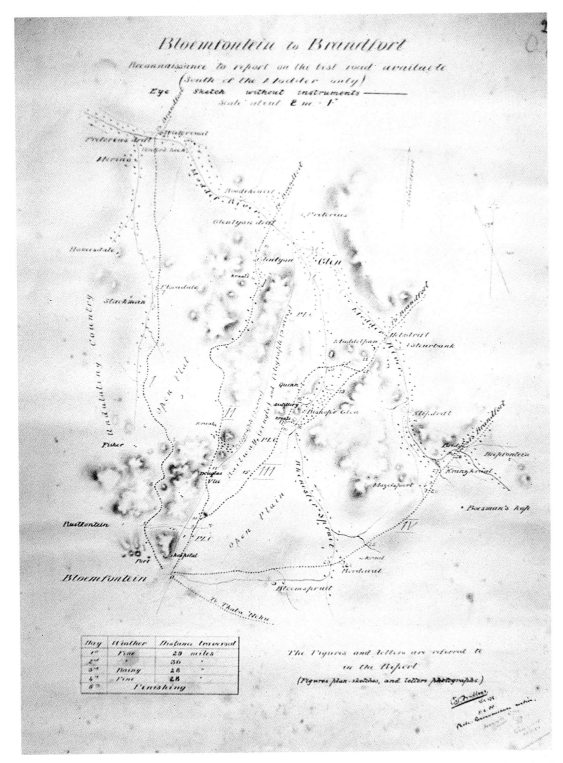

Left **Map of the territory between Bloemfontein and Brandfort prepared by Lieutenant C. H. Foulkes, RE, dated 5 April 1900. The Engineers were responsible for supplying the deficiency of mapping and were making use of such devices as a Newman and Guardia 5 x 4in. twin lens camera with a telephoto lens.**
(RE.MFME BW18/22)

far as the C-in-C who, on observing a tin clearly marked 'Van Houten's Cocoa' masquerading as ammunition, simply remarked, 'Well, they mark it very funnily!'

On 12 May they entered Kroonstadt where a ten day halt was needed to make good the railway and bring up supplies, then on they went with little pause to cross the Vaal on 24 May. There they found Botha and De la Rey holding the hills west and south of Johannesburg. The main infantry force, 7th and 11th Divisions, moved east of the city while Hamilton crossed to the west to join French. Here, south-west of the city, overlooking the Klip River, the Boers were in occupation of Doornkop, the place of Jameson's surrender in the famous Raid (see map on p.127). The two generals conferred, and found that while French

Below **Venette Kopje Fort, past which Eloff's men came in the attack of 12 May. Drawing by Sergeant F. J. Stebbins after a sketch by Captain R. B. Christie, Cape Police. Dated 24 March 1900 and countersigned by Major Alexander Godley.** (RE5201.16/9. MFME BW19/1)

Bottom **A drawing of Maxim Fort which Stebbins was allowed to make without assistance. Dated 17 March 1900.** (RE5201.16/15. MFME BW19/4)

had supplies for some days and thus could afford time to outflank the position, Hamilton was down to one day's rations, though it is possible that he favoured moving directly forward in any case. French took the cavalry round to the west while Hamilton launched the infantry against the ridge. On the left was Major-general Bruce-Hamilton's 21st Brigade with the City Imperial Volunteers leading the advance, supported by the 1st Derbyshire Regiment to their left and the 1st Cameron Highlanders on their right. Major-general Smith-Dorrien's 19th Brigade was on the right with the 1st Gordon Highlanders in the van, the 2nd Duke of Cornwall's Light Infantry to their left and the Royal Canadian Regiment on the right. The CIV moved into attack cautiously, moving by bounds, one section giving cover to the next, and covered by artillery supporting fire. The Gordons advanced in two long lines against the supposed summit line, crossing an area burnt black against which their khaki showed clearly. Having reached the ridge they found it, as so often in this war, a false crest and had to push on again

against heavy Mauser fire to clear the hill with the bayonet. The casualties of the CIV were relatively light, but the Gordons lost heavily with 97 casualties, 18 of them fatal.

East of the city the concern was to take the ground swiftly enough to prevent the rolling stock being moved away up the line to Pretoria, for it was badly needed to supplement the supply service. Indeed, the American scout, Major Burnham, who had succeeded in escaping from De Wet, had been sent behind Boer lines to blow the bridges as the British approached, remaining hidden in an ant-bear's hole with an African companion. They blew the line on a curve and blew it again when the Boers repaired the damage. He reports

'Our performance was essentially successful. A large quantity of most valuable rolling stock and many engines were captured by the British ... and were put to immediate use in bringing up supplies for both the town population and the British troops.'

With a skirmish or two, the town was taken by 2 June.

THE RELIEF OF MAFEKING

As the advance on the Transvaal began in the centre, two forces were on the move away to the west, striking for Mafeking. From the north Colonel Herbert Plumer with his Rhodesians and from the south Colonel Bryan Mahon with a flying column of about 1,000 men from the Imperial Light Horse, the Kimberley Mounted Corps with a small number of infantrymen and four guns of M Battery, Royal Horse Artillery and some machine-guns crossed the Vaal on 4 May. Plumer was trying for a second time; he had been badly mauled at the end of March. As a result Baden-Powell seriously contemplated withdrawing from the town in secret and surrendering it to the Boers. Now he daily awaited news of the progress of the relieving forces.

On the morning of 12 May, before sunrise, gunfire from the north-east woke the people of Mafeking, Baden-Powell amongst them. His first reaction was to telephone Lieutenant H. T. Mackenzie, commander of the 'Black Watch', the armed Africans who were in the forts on the south-west, and found them still in place. He then contacted Major Alexander Godley on the west, just as a messenger arrived, and was able to give Godley the news that a Boer force had entered the *stadt*, Mafikeng, taken it, and pushed on to capture the British South Africa Police Fort on the western edge of the European township, Mafeking. Orders were issued to close up the western defences to prevent reinforcement of the intruders. It soon became clear that Commandant Sarel Eloff, a grandson of Kruger and second in command to Snyman, had led the attack and was now in the BSAP fort with about 150 men, three-fifths of his attacking force. They were quickly surrounded, Baden-Powell thinning the

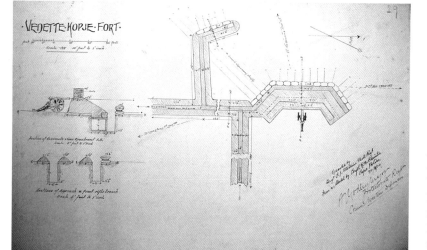

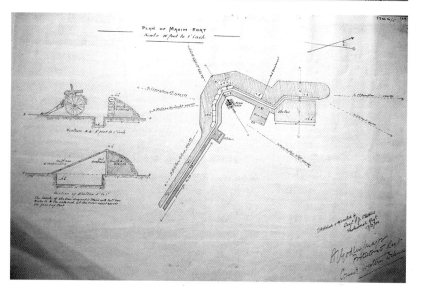

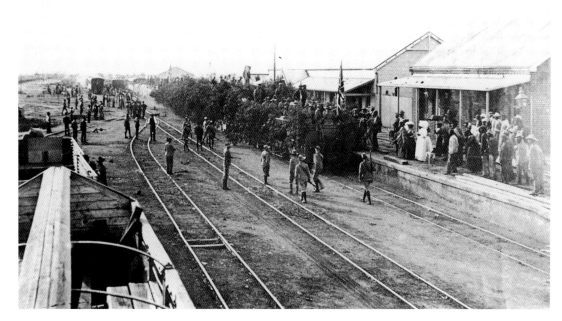

Left **The first train in from the north, 24 May 1900, after the relief of Mafeking.** (McG. MMKP5149)

garrison on the east and south to find the men. Colonel Hore, three officers and 23 other ranks were prisoners in Eloff's hands, as also was Nurse A. M. Craufurd who had been caught up in the original attack.

Godley wasted no time in dealing with the Boers in Mafikeng. Indeed, the Baralong might well have done the job without assistance. Fearing the dangers of shooting his own side, Godley was content to drive the attackers out of the town rather than to kill or capture them. Nonetheless Boer casualties included nine killed or wounded and some 25 prisoners here. At the BSAP fort the captives' number had been augmented by Angus Hamilton, correspondent of *The Times*, who had approached thinking the men around the fort were British. He reported Eloff's courtesy and steadiness as the long day passed and no reinforcements came. Towards evening, having lost a number of men sent vainly to summon help, Eloff suffered the defection of yet more of his force. He went to the storeroom, where his prisoners were held, and asked Hore to accept his surrender and put a stop to the incessant rifle fire from the British. The Boer attempt, unsupported by Snyman, had failed.

Edward Ross, an auctioneer, had been recruited into the Town Guard early on, and complained of his treatment.

'These [he and his like] are men who hold very high positions in the town, and who are now living in the trenches and doing 'Tommy Atkins' work for no pay and less thanks... most of the men in one of the redoubts talk of getting up a petition and working for the removal of their commander.'

The tone was rather different after the events of 12 May.

'I can assure you it was indeed a lesson to all who saw him [Baden-Powell]. I had that luck. He stood there at the corner of his offices, the coolest of cucumbers possible, but his orders rattled out like the rip of a Maxim... [It] shewed us the ideal soldier, and what the British officer can be and is in moments of extreme peril.'

No doubt both passages of Ross's memoirs have a proportion of truth.

On 13 May Mahon's column had a brush with Commandant P. J. Liebenberg's commando some 60 miles (100km) south of Mafeking, losing five killed and 21 wounded, but throwing off the Boers. On 15 May Mahon and Plumer met at Massibi, west of the besieged town, and two days later encountered more serious resistance to their progress. De la Rey had brought another 1,000 men to reinforce Liebenberg and Snyman had detached 200 to assist. They fought on the Molopo River at Israel's Farm, some 8 miles (13km) north-west of Mafeking. British intelligence was good and Mahon put his trust in it, calculating that De la Rey had spread his forces wide to give the impression of even greater number than he actually had. A month before Major Joseph Hudon had been ordered to take C Battery, Royal Canadian Artillery, to join Plumer, by way of Beira and Bulawayo. Within 20 hours of his arrival he was marching with the Rhodesian Field Force, and now the Canadians were able to make their vital contribution, 180 rounds that, in the course of four hours, overcame four Boer gun positions. The infantry, veterans of the Natal campaign, worked their way forward in rushes supported by rifle and artillery covering fire. In reserve, men of the Queensland Mounted Infantry, chafed at being

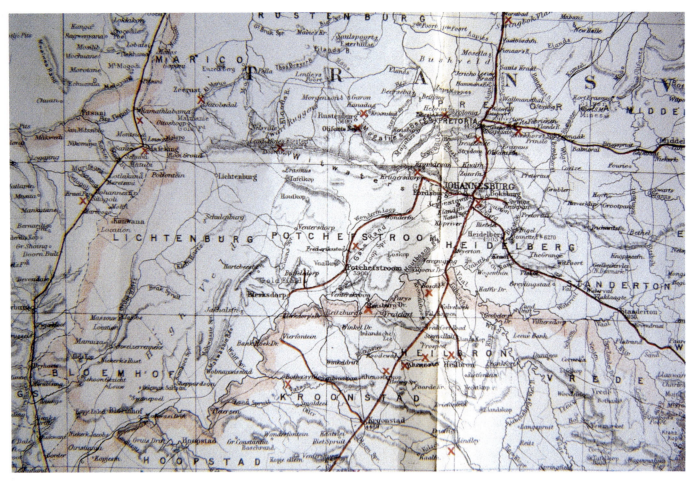

Above **Map of the Transvaal
from Mafeking to
Johannesburg and south to
the Vaal River, the border
with the Orange Free State,
from *With the Flag to
Pretoria*. Major actions are
marked with a cross.**

excluded from the battle. When they saw the English start their final bayonet charge they could stand still no longer and were soon running side by side with the attackers. The Boers broke and the way to Mafeking lay open.

Corporal Ernest Warby, from Sydney, was with the Imperial Light Horse and described the day.

'At dusk we had the Boers beaten. Then our Major Karri Davies called for volunteers to ride with him into the town … You can bet I was in that lot. We galloped all the way, striking across country… The first challenge we got was an English voice: "Halt who goes there." We yelled out: "The Imperial Light Horse."

'… Soon we were met by men galloping out to learn what was up. When we got to headquarters the crowd swarmed around us, everyone wanting to shake hands at once. Then they struck up "Rule Britannia" and the National Anthem.'

The news was greeted in England, Australia and Canada with an enthusiasm far greater than the strategic importance of this little town justified, a reaction that has encouraged myth and myth-breaking on an equally exaggerated scale. For morale the relief was excellent, the last of the Boers' initial objectives was back in British hands.

THE FLANKS

Left and right of the main thrust for Johannesburg, Methuen and Hamilton were clearing the ground and numerous minor actions flared across the country as the British arrived and then moved on once more. Like building sandcastles on the beach, the short-term effect was outstanding, but the tide of Boer occupation soon obliterated the achievements. The areas concerned were what De Wet called the granaries, the Ladybrand, Ficksburg and Bethlehem regions of the Orange Free State and the Potchefstroom area in Transvaal. The harvest was good that year, as De Wet wrote:

'As the men were away on commando the Kaffirs reaped the corn under the supervision of the Boer women and where Kaffirs were not obtainable the women did the work with their own hands, and were assisted by their little sons and daughters. The women provided such a large supply, that had not the English burnt the corn by the thousand sacks, the war could have been continued.'

The infantry suffered most in this process. Lieutenant Barton records that, having left Boshof on 14 May, the Northamptons marched 225 miles (362km) in 17 days. The column's 200 ox-wagons filled seven miles (11km) of road. The kit of the men was carried as follows:

'2 Blankets, carried in Wagons

1 Waterproof sheet, carried on the man

1 Great Coat, carried in Wagons with the shirt & socks
    in pockets

1 pair canvas shoes, carried in Waterproof sheet on man

1 pair socks, carried in Great Coat pocket on wagon

1 Jersey, carried in waterproof sheet on man

1 Flannel shirt, carried in Great Coat pocket on wagon'

His own kit, he says, was down to 35lbs (16kg), thus:

'Waterproof Valise	10lbs
Bag blanket	6lbs
Clothing – 1 shirt, 2pr socks, 1 sweater, 1 pr. pants, 2 cholera belts, 1 Balaclava cap, 2 coloured & 2 silk handkerchiefs, in canvas bag to keep off damp	4lbs
Toilet bag – 1 Sponge, 1 towel, 1 Razor, 1 shaving brush, 1 Hair brush, 1 Tooth brush, 1 Box tooth powder, 2 cakes soap, 1 looking glass, Nail nippers, Lantern folding	3lbs
Clothes – 1 Khaki Coat, 1 trousers, 1 felt hat	4lbs
1 pr Boots, 1 pr canvas shoes	3lbs
Writing case, Prayer book, House wife	3lbs
Canvas water bucket & water bag	2lbs
	35lbs

'In addition I carry on the march my Waterproof with
a knitted Cardigan vest rolled inside weighing 5½ lbs.'

The advance took Barton to Hoopstadt, the Vaal
River and Bothaville and then off to the east,
Kroonstad and Lindley. Piet de Wet, like his brother,
seemed not to appreciate that the Boers were beaten in
the Free State and when he found the 13th Imperial
Yeomanry near Lindley, he fought them. Under the
command of Lieutenant-colonel Basil Spragge, the
force included such blue-bloods as the Earl of
Longford, Viscount Ennismore and the Earl of
Leitrim. This did not impress Piet. Those who were
not killed were taken prisoner. Methuen's column,
despite the hard marching, was too late to rescue
them.

Christiaan De Wet was also busy. He surrounded
a Heilbron-bound food convoy, some 55 wagons, at
Roodewal on the Rhenoster River. They were guarded
by a force of 160 men of the Highland Brigade. They

Below **Map of the Orange
River Colony (sic) between
Kroonstad and the
Drakensberg Mountains to
the south-east, including
Senekal, Biddulphsberg and
Bethlehem and the Caledon
River basin east of Ficksburg.
From *With the Flag to
Pretoria*.**

Below **The infantry marched in South Africa as it had never marched before. The distances they covered were prodigious and the care of their feet was essential. Here the King's Royal Rifles prepare for foot inspection.**

(McM. MFME BW11/14)

had no option but to surrender. This was, however, a side-show; what De Wet was really after was the great accumulation of supplies at Roodewal Station, where it had been building up pending the repair of the bridge over the Rhenoster River. With four 75-mm Krupps and a quick-firing gun, De Wet's force had a substantial advantage over the ill-prepared British. He divided it into three parties to attack the three British camps and took the 4th Derbyshires prisoner as well as various others connected with the railway and postal services. The mail bags were raided and looted by both the Boers and the British. The Boers were so keen on booty that it was with great difficulty that De Wet managed to carry away the .303 ammunition, important because he was increasingly using captured British rifles, and ammunition for captured field guns which was later hidden on his farm at Roodepoort nearby. The torment of the British was to continue here despite an attempt under Kitchener's personal command to put a stop to it, during which the Boers nearly trapped Kitchener himself when they stopped a train at Leeuwspruit Bridge, north of the Rhenoster.

Lieutenant-general Sir Leslie Rundle had been shadowing Roberts's advance with his 8th Division,

moving up behind the main force over on the eastern flank, through ThabaNchu and generally north-eastwards by way of Koppieskraal. Yet further east Major-general E. Y. Brabant moved alongside with men of the Colonial Division. The objective was to prevent the Boers, under General A. I. De Villiers, re-occupying the south-eastern Free State. A company of the 8th Division's 11th Imperial Yeomanry under Major H. S. Dalbiac was sent in advance of Rundle's main body towards Senekal on 25 May and entered the little town late in the morning, taking up positions on the east to cover the Bethlehem road. A Boer attack in the afternoon resulted in the death of Dalbiac and others, the surrender of 13 men and the surrounding of the remainder of the force in the town. A message had been sent to Rundle and the approach of reinforcements and the artillery led to a Boer retreat and the full occupation of Senekal. Just another little incident along the way, and another four British graves in the local cemetery, as well as one Boer.

The 8th's headquarters moved to Senekal and probing patrols moved east. The Imperial Yeomanry ran into Boers at Tafelkop, a prominent hill off the Rosendal road, losing another man killed. When, a

couple of days later, Colonel Spragge sent a message from Lindley appealing for assistance for the 13th Imperial Yeomanry, Rundle decided the diversion of his force from its easterly route was not justified, but that a demonstration of force would detain De Villiers in the Senekal area and thus take pressure off Spragge. It did nothing to help Spragge, in fact, and was to bestow no benefit on Rundle and what is more, Rundle's telegraph to Brabant informing him of the scheme was intercepted by the Boers.

The Boers were in occupation of a semi-circle of kopjes astride the Rosendal and Bethlehem roads about 6 miles (10km) east, Tafelberg in the south, Platkop in the centre and Biddulphsberg on the north, this last being a substantial flat-topped hill. Rundle decided to avoid the potential trap by out-flanking the hills to the north, and at 4am on 29 May his advance proceeded. Three companies of the East Yorkshires with two guns occupied Gwarriekop on the Senkal road behind which the British had camped the previous night. A company of the Imperial Yeomanry covered Tafelkop and another the main Bethlehem road, while the main force, the West Kents, the Grenadier and the Scots Guards, marched off to the northern side of Biddulphsberg with three companies of the Yeomanry and 2 and 79 Batteries, Royal Field Artillery. De Villiers moved his men to wrap themselves round the northern end of the hill where they concealed themselves on the lower slopes and set up a 75mm Krupp in a stone cattle kraal and a pom-

pom nearby close to the Erasmus's farm. Just to the north 34 men of the Ladybrand commando under Field-cornet P. Ferreira occupied the ditches along the roadside and, away to the northeast there was another Krupp. The British approach swung round to close with the hill from the northwest under the cover of shellfire from the Field Artillery, while near the foot of the hill the tall, dry grass was now ablaze, though whether by accident or design is unclear. The Boer riflemen held their fire. The Boer artillery was silenced by the British shell fire and the British infantry drew yet closer to the hill. When they were some 1,200 yards (1,100m) away the Krupp opened up again, together with Mauser fire from the hill and the enfilading ditch postions. The wind had been blowing from the east, giving the British some cover from view, but now it turned and the westerly blew the fire towards the soldiers. Flames six feet (1.8m) high barred their way. The nimble leaped through to face Boer bullets, but the wounded had no means of escape and died in the blaze. Covered by elements of the Scots Guards and West Kents, the British started to retire and, seeing this, De Villiers and his men charged forward. The attack was repulsed and De Villiers wounded in the jaw. The British withdrawal became complete when the news of the 12th Infantry Brigade's arrival in Senekal and the 8th Division's redeployment to Ficksburg became known. As the retirement took place repeated forays were made to pull men from the flames. Forty-seven men died and 130 were wounded on the British side while the Boer losses amounted to three wounded and one killed. One died of wounds. De Villiers was so severely hurt that the Boers were unable to treat him and asked the British to do so. He was taken to Senekal, but the efforts of the doctors were in vain.

BULLER ON THE MOVE

The Boers had withdrawn from the environs of Ladysmith to establish a line on the Biggarsberg mountains, north of Elandslaagte and south of Glencoe, where they had some 16,000 men and 30 guns. Buller, meanwhile, was stuck at Ladysmith, fretting against the inertia imposed on him by Roberts. The Boers took advantage of this inactivity to transfer men to the Free State, but still had half of the original number there by the end of April. On 5 April the 5th Division took up positions at Elandslaagte, the 16th Battery, Southern Division, Royal Garrison Artillery with its 5in. guns making new emplacements facing north on the hilltop so dashingly taken in the early days of the war. On 10

Above **A British 5in. gun as used by the Royal Garrison Artillery. This example is mounted on a makeshift carriage and is on diplay at the War Museum of the Boer Republics, Bloemfontein.** (MFME BW15/2)

Right **Looking north-east over a substantial British emplacement at Elandslaagte.** (MFME BW9/3)

Main picture **Biddulphsberg from the north. The British attacked the hill from the right of this road and the Ladybrand men occupied ditches to the left.** (MFME BW15/6)

Above **The Biggarsberg from the hill taken by the Gordons and the ILH at Elandslaagte, with the Boer Memorial on the next hill. The gun emplacements were built by the British in the advance of 1900.** (MFME BW9/4)

April an attack was mounted on the British 2nd Division camp nearby and an artillery duel followed. The British assumed it was a device to precipitate an impulsive counter-attack, but there was less science behind it than they thought. Deneys Reitz was on the opposing front.

'This much-criticized affair was to have been carried out by three thousand Transvaalers in conjunction with an equal force of Freestaters … Prinsloo had telegraphed to General Botha at the last moment to say he and his officers were attending a cattle sale at Harrismith … and were therefore unable to be present… General Botha had to change his plans and content himself with a mere demonstration …'

That was the end of Reitz's service in Natal. He and his brother departed for the Transvaal to oppose the British advance against their home country, joining Commandant Malan's Afrikander Cavalry Corps, the ACC.

Buller's patience eventually gave way to active pursuit of the enemy and, on 10 May, the 2nd Division swung east to outflank the Biggarsberg while the 5th Division pushed up the railway line. By 16 May Dundonald was in Glencoe and by 17 May Buller was in Newcastle. The Boers fell back to Laing's Nek to hold the pass into the Transvaal where they

had enjoyed their great success of the previous war. Here, under the gaze of Majuba Hill, the railway passed through a tunnel, easily blocked.

On 2 June Buller's overtures eventually resulted in a meeting with the Boer commander, Louis Botha's brother, Christiaan, at Laing's Nek when it was suggested that further fighting was futile. The Afrikaner agreed to consult his government and a three-day truce was agreed. During this time Buller was consolidating his positons for his next move, so nothing was lost when the peace proposal was rejected. On 7 June the two 5in. guns of the right-half 16th Battery, Southern Division, RGA were moved to the summit of Inkwelo, south of Majuba, by night. The attempt to haul them up with oxen failed when a gun overturned and fell back, oxen and all, some 30 feet, so the poor infantry had to turn out in the middle of the night and sweat the weapons up with ropes. The left-half battery was positioned to the north-west of Van Wyk Hill. At 10am on 8 June they opened fire on Botha's Pass. With this artillery support and for a loss of 15 casualties the pass was taken and that night, in the winter cold, Buller bivouacked with his troops. The bastion of Laing's Nek was outflanked and, although stiff resistance was still be to met and overcome at Alleman's Nek, the

Boers fled. Trooper Fred Marshall from Gundagai was now with the Maxim Detachment and had a full day at Alleman's Nek.

'… a helio message was flashed for two guns to assist … on the right flank three miles away. We limbered up and galloped away at full speed, arriving just in time to stop the Boers from working round our left flank. We were soon in action and under a withering fire drove the Boers back … When the Boers were … beaten we reconnoitred the position and found 142 dead … The day following this decisive engagement our men buried 420 Boers. It was a terrible day's work, but it cleared the way to Volksrust.'

When Buller got back to the railway on 12 June the hope of trapping 4,500 burghers was gone, but the main Boer position had been abandoned without a shot fired. The work to clear the tunnel and bring the railway back into service started at once.

Buller's and Roberts's forces met at last on 4 July, by which time the former had occupied Standerton, and the British optimistically felt two or three months would see the end of the war.

AFTER PRETORIA

Pretoria fell on 5 June 1900. Both capitals were now in British hands and that seemed to be that. But

Below **Intelligence Division, War Office, map No.1223, sheet 2, April 1897; the country north of Newcastle. Inkwelo is at N7, Van Wyk Hill at L10 and Botha's Pass at K10.** (TM. MFME BWMF5)

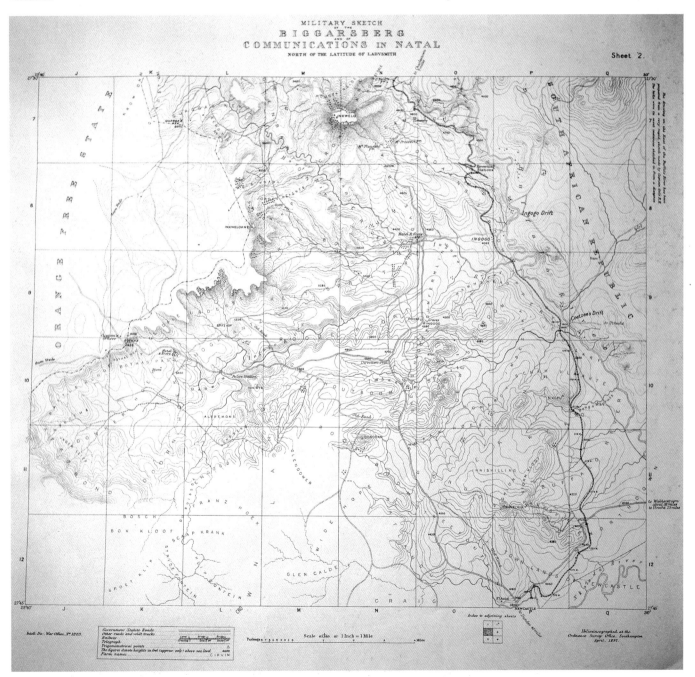

President Kruger moved his capital to a railway carriage, went to Machadodorp, and the war went on. The railway the Boers still controlled was the Delagoa Bay line, although the British could be forgiven for feeling that they almost controlled a good deal more as De Wet set about his raids. Through the line to the east coast the Boers could still hope to receive supplies and aid from outside. Botha established a front on a range of hills some 16 miles (25km) east of Pretoria through Diamond Hill and Elands Poort, the gap through which the railway passed, and on along the hills south of the railway and the road, bending gently westwards, manned by some 6,000 men and 22 guns. Roberts's troops were reduced by fatigue and illness and the cavalry by lack of horses. He had about 14,000 men, a third of them mounted, and artillery numbering 70 guns, six of them heavy. As usual Roberts was planning to demonstrate against the centre and put in his heavy blows on the flanks; Botha planned for just such an attack.

General French was on the left and his attack of 11 June was soon pinned down on the Kameelpoort road by De la Rey's men. General Broadwood's cavalry Brigade, with Ridley's Mounted Infantry on his left and Gordon's on the right, found itself thrusting into the angle of the hills and enfiladed from both sides. Two guns of Q Battery, Royal Horse Artillery came into action to clear the way and, most unusually, were the subject of a mounted charge by Boers. The 12th Lancers counter-charged, putting the Boers to flight, but losing their commanding officer, Lord Airlie, just as he was shouting to an NCO who was expressing his

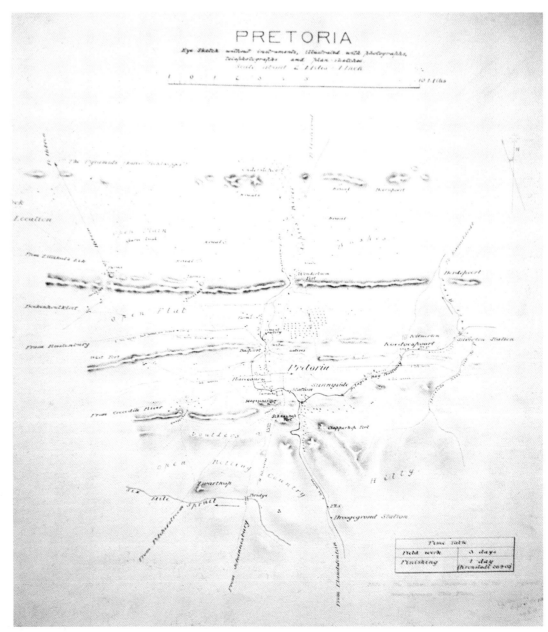

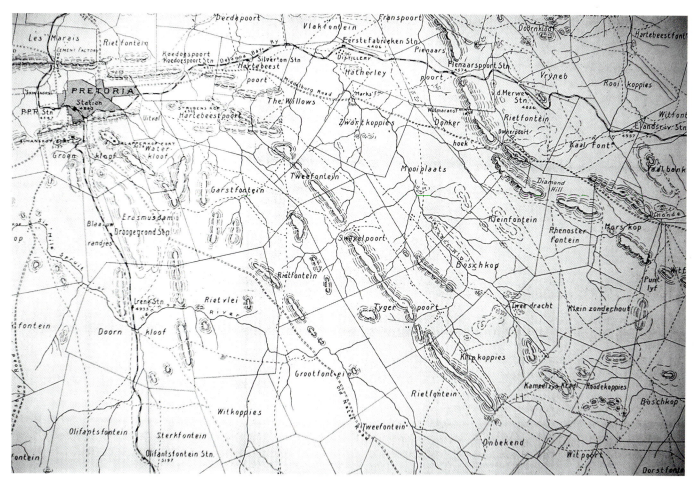

opinion of his opponents, 'Sergeant, sergeant, moderate your language!' The Lancers withdrew and the Boers came on again, this time to be sent running by the Household Cavalry.

In the centre Ian Hamilton's infantry were doing little better against Diamond Hill itself. The City Imperial Volunteers on the right and the 1st Royal Sussex and 1st Derbyshire Regiments on the left moved forward from cover to cover, supported by artillery fire, and took a first ridge, only to discover another, yet higher, stood beyond it. In the failing light they withdrew to the cover of the first ridge and settled for the night. The next day the infantry battle continued with Hamilton's men reinforced by the Guards Brigade from Pole-Carew's 11th Division and a lodgement on the hilltop was obtained with the help of the 82nd Field Battery. The British were still overlooked by Boers on yet higher hillocks and, on the north, French was so hard-pressed that De la Rey felt confident of being able to turn the British flank. He had sent to Botha for support to attempt this when Colonel H. B. De Lisle's Mounted Corps intervened. It had been in reserve behind the Tigerspoort Hills south of Silverton to the west, but had moved forward on the morning of 12 June and, at 2pm, De Lisle sent it against the Boer left and the dominant kopje above

Rhenosterfontein farm. The 6th Regular Mounted Infantry seized a position at the foot of the hill and the New South Wales Mounted Rifles, supported by the West Australians, finished the job. Trooper Allan Cameron was in the charge to the farm:

'We were ordered to look to our girths and then the order came to mount and extend 50 yards [46m]. We then galloped in the direction of the kopje where the Boers were. We had some pom-poms covering our advance, and it was not long before puffs of dust began to fly off the ground, letting us know the Boers were firing at us.'

The pom-poms were sent forward to the cover of the farm wall and the NSWMI dismounted and moved to the foot of the hill, a steep slope up which they scrambled, at first sheltered by the slope from Boer fire. The order was given to fix bayonets and charge. Trooper E. M. Hoffman recalled:

'A real colonial yell went up when we got the Boers running, carrying their wounded with them. They had an easy slope to go down, so they were soon mounted and out of range.'

Two Australian officers died in the attack, Lieutenant W. R. Harriott and Lieutenant P. W. C. Drage. Banjo Paterson wrote of them:

'Harriott and Drage stood up, urging the men on, calling them by name. The men implored them to lie down, but they took no heed. They actually got their pipes and filled them, while the Boer bullets whizzed past and splatted in little grey patches on the rocks.'

Allan Cameron was wounded.

'Lieutenant Harriott and I with a couple more were making a general rush forward together, when down I went on my face with a terrific shock in my chest. I thought I was cooked. The poor Harriott went down with a groan… I never saw the rifle fire so hot. It used to burst overhead like thunder and you could hear it buzzing amongst the rocks.'

With the loss of the kopje at the south-eastern corner of his position, it was clear to Botha that they would not be able to hold, and they therefore withdrew during the night. It was a British victory, but a massive boost to Boer morale, for it had taken two days to shake their hold on Diamond Hill and, after the long, miserable series of defeats and flights through the Free State and into Transvaal, the battle had restored their self-respect. The prospect of peace faded.

The fight had depleted the slender reserves of ammunition available to Roberts and he was in no hurry to pursue, although the Australians showed more enthusiasm and caught a small band of Boers at Bronkhorstspruit, Freda Schlosberg's home town. The flow of retreating Boers caused Freda's family, now removed further east, problems.

'... *four men came to our house and to our surprise one of them began reading in loud and aggressive tones a "proclamation"... [in] the following terms:*

"'Commandos are ordered to commandeer all edibles, cattle and horses, as well as produce and anything that might be useful to the enemy, giving owners receipts. All provisions, cattle and horses and other things which cannot be taken must be destroyed.'"

They argued, wept, pleaded and managed to soften some hearts, but much of their food, all their horses and cattle and some of their mules went. The rest of the civilian population were treated similarly. Clearly a scorched earth policy had been adopted, officially or unofficially, by the retreating Boers. A good deal of the destruction was wrought by virtually starving and leaderless bands, many of them foreign volunteers. Freda's father recounted the experiences of the people of Bronkhorstspruit where the Irish had plundered his house and the Italians had burnt down the houses of Mr Becker and Mr Erasmus, both away on commando.

In the north-eastern Free State Roberts was conducting a three-sided advance intended to entrap President Steyn, Christiaan De Wet and Marthinus

Prinsloo with the commandos of the Free State against the Drakensberg Mountains and the Basutoland (Lesotho) border where the Wittebergen and the Roodebergen were shrouded in winter snow. Here were the Brandwater Basin and the valley of the Little Caledon river, open to the south-west by Commando Nek, to the north-west by Wet Nek, and to the north by Slabbert's and Retief's Neks. The Little Caledon is reached through Slaapkranz and may be left by Naauwpoort Nek to the north and Golden Gate to the east, the road to Natal. De Wet divided the Boer force into three divisions, the first of which he commanded and which included Steyn and the apparatus of government. Danie Theron and his 80 scouts and Captain Gideon Scheepers and his scouts were also with him. As planned this division slipped away through Slabbert's Nek on the night of 15 to 16 July. Paul Roux commanded the second division which was to head in the direction of Bloemfontein while General Crowther had the third, intended to go north of Bethlehem.

After De Wet's departure disputes broke out and on 17 July Prinsloo was elected commander of the remaining burghers. While this disagreement was disorganising the Boers, the British, by chance, started their advance. Major-general Arthur Paget's 20th

Below **The pom-pom train of the 4th Mounted Infantry**
(Major G. N. M. Darwell, NRA. MFME BW1/32)

Progress was slow, but the Boers were too disorganised to offer stout resistance and withdrew in the night. Then Childers entered the country beyond,

'... an immense amphitheatre of rich, undulating pasture-land, with a white farm here and there, half-hidden in trees. Beyond rose tier on tier of hills, ending on snow-clad mountain peaks.'

Lovat's Scouts had reconnoitred Retief's Nek so well that Hunter had a sound knowledge of the Boer positions, without which he might have failed. It was, in any case, a tough fight. The Black Watch were held up on the ridge and were reinforced that night by the Highland Light Infantry and Rimington's Mounted Infantry. At dawn the Seaforth Highlanders also came up and, after one of the British 5in. guns had silenced the Boer Creusot, drove the Boers off at bayonet-point supported by covering fire from the Black Watch. The northern passes were now both in British hands. Ian Hamilton's depleted force had difficulty in dealing with the eastern passes and General Olivier and men of the Harrismith commando got away through Golden Gate before the gap could be plugged. Meanwhile Rundle had been coming up by way of Fouriesburg and Slaapkrantz, which was taken on 29 July. The Boers were shut in.

After some negotiation and prevarication, the Boers surrendered. Prinsloo was doubtful of the extent his authority would be recognised but by 31 July the more reluctant had become 'hands-uppers' as De Wet would contemptuously refer to them. Banjo Paterson witnessed the scene.

'About dusk we saw the Boer army with wagons and guns, toiling along a huge spur of the hills, coming in to surrender ... The burghers varied in years from grey-bearded men to mere boys between 11 and 12 years of age. With them came many women and children almost black with sun and exposure. They had been crying and they formed a pitiful procession ...'

The haul was 4,500 men and thousands of sheep and cattle. The arms and ammunition were handed in to form a mighty bonfire, the mark of which scars the slope of Surrender Hill to this day.

Above **A Boer burgher and a man of the ZARP (South African Republic Police) captured by the British. The officer still carries his sword and one of the men of the Natal Carbineers has a combined bandolier and carbine bucket.**

(Gerry Embleton, from Men-at-Arms 303 *Boer Wars (2) 1898–1902*)

Right **Still to be found with a casual kick, rusty rounds, Martini cartridge bases and twisted gun fittings at Surrender Hill.** (MFME BW12/16)

Brigade, with the 2nd Northamptons and 4th South Staffordshires as reinforcements, closed Slabbert's Nek on 16 July, just too late to catch De Wet. Lieutenant-general Sir Leslie Rundle closed Commando Nek and Lieutenant-general Sir Archibald Hunter, with MacDonald's Highland Brigade and Lovat's Scouts went for Retief's Nek. Ian Hamilton watched the exits to the east. On 23 July Slabbert's Nek was attacked. Erskine Childers, Clerk to the House of Commons, later to write *The Riddle of the Sands* and eventually die as a member of the Irish Repbublican Army before a firing squad, was serving as a driver in the Honorable Artillery Company Battery of the City Imperial Volunteers. They had, in the relief of Lindley three weeks earlier, fired the first shot on foreign soil in the 350 years' existence of the H A C He wrote of the nek:

'... stretching back into the mountains like a great pass road, bordered with battlements of precipitous rock ... On these are Boer trenches, tier above tier ... It looks like an impregnable position.'

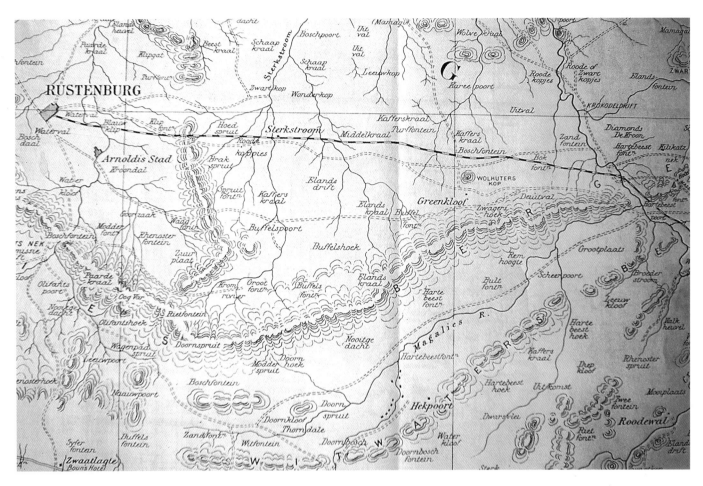

Above **Detail from IDWO map No. 1367, Rustenburg, published in 1900.** (BL E54.4 [1])

After Diamond Hill De la Rey and Jan Smuts, with about 7,000 Transvaal men and 19 guns, made a wide swing to the north and west of Pretoria to the Magaliesberg mountains. Roberts had a new front to contend with, though the concept of a front was becoming redundant. Rustenburg had to be retaken by the New South Wales Citizens' Bushmen on 7 July and on 11 July 189 men of the Scots Greys and the Lincolns surrendered to De la Rey at Zilikat's Nek. Methuen was called north from the Free State and French back from the east to clear the area from the south and north respectively. The 2nd Northamptons were on the move again. Lieutenant Barton wrote:

'15 July … The Northamptonshire Regiment with the RE & the section RA are to entrain at Honing Spruit [north of Kroonstadt] tonight … 16 July, Monday … the rolling stock consisted of a number of short open bogie trucks into which men were packed 26 men per truck … With the 2nd train came the business of getting the mules into the cattle trucks … many were more carried than led … No one can properly enjoy a train until he has done five or six hundred miles on his own feet & constantly seen the railway without being able to use it.'

The three trains on which this column travelled went by way of Elandsfontein, Johannesburg and then west to Krugersdorp. At 2.15pm on 18 July they were on the move in the company of Smith-Dorrien's column to counter the threat to Rustenburg represented by De la Rey's occupation of Olifant's Nek.

'An entirely new country, round, rugged, precipitous hills, deep winding valleys in every direction. To catch well mounted parties of men knowing the country seemed a task almost too much for any Regular army.

'19 July … Great tactical schemes had been planned to get the Boers between two columns but the enemy instead of trying to defend a strong position which he was reported to be holding cleared off without waiting for us, a few shots only being fired … The country now became mountainous instead of hilly while parts of it resembled Wales very closely, though without so much wood still there were more trees than on the Veldt. In the evening we camped by a real cultivated farm & the place & scenery really was beautiful.'

On 21 July they moved on to contest the Boer occupation of Olifant's Hoek, marching along the Rustenburg road to the foot of the

'Magaliesburg Mountains which run east-west with precipitous sides practically inaccesible for tactical purposes some 1,000 feet [300m] above the undulating plain … about 9am the first shots came echoing down the mountains & the column got ready for battle.'

Above **Captain Ripley leads E Company, 2nd Northamptons, towards Olifant's Nek. Lieutenant Barton, from whose journal this comes, is to be seen at Ripley's elbow.** (NRA. MFME BW 1/7)

Right **Captain Pritchard of the 2nd Northamptons at the ruined laager of Elands River Post, so determinedly defended by the Australians under Colonel Hore.** (NRA. MFME BW 1/11)

the 5th on it & a little higher up we found a Yeomanry corporal lying with a bullet through his head, quite lifeless.'

While the status of Rustenburg had been in question, supplies had piled up at Elands River Post 40 miles (64km) to the west of the town and west of Magato Nek, on the road to Zeerust. The Post was set up on a low kopje close to the road and the river in a valley some two to three miles (3 to 5 km) wide, and a number of outlying kopjes were also occupied. Baden-Powell, now a Major-general, sent Colonel H. P. Airey with 300 Australians to 'brush aside' the Boers blocking the road at the Koster River. The force was ambushed and pinned down all through 22 July, being relieved only when a young English woman from a nearby farm, Miss Bach, rode for help. The garrison at Elands River Post was under Lieutenant-colonel C. O. Hore who had come through the Mafeking siege. He had, on 25 July, 105 New South Wales Citizens' Bushmen, 141 3rd Queensland Mounted Infantry, two Tasmanian Bushmen, 42 Victorian Bushmen, 9 Western Australian Bushmen and 201 Rhodesian Volunteers. That day he learned of an intended Boer attack.

Attempts to make the Australians dig defensive trenches met with good-humoured non-compliance. A detail under Corporal C. W. Norton, Victorian Bushmen, managed a six-inch (15cm) scrape in a day's work, embellished with a large slate inscribed: 'Erected to the memory of the Victorians, who were compelled

The Northamptons were not, that day, to fight. The Boers soon left their positions and the advance became much like a pleasant country walk.

'... Magnificent butterflies just coming out with the spring were flitting among the rocks, one associated the scene with a peaceful holiday in Wales or Yorkshire till as we climbed up there came down a stretcher with one of

Left **A distant view of Olifant's
Nek, from Barton's journal.**
(NRA. MFME BW1/3)

to dig this trench. Fort Funk, 3 August 1900'. It was decided the Post was too exposed and that the men should be withdrawn. On Friday 3 August Lieutenant-general Sir Frederick Carrington left Zeerust with 1,000 men, six guns and four pom-poms on the way to the east. He was expected at Elands River on Sunday. At daybreak on Saturday the Boers shelled the Post, cutting down the animals in the exposed enclave. Men ran for their trenches. Trooper H. E. M. Tully, Western Australian Bushmen, wrote:

'... there was a perfect hail of bullets and shells. North, south, east, and west they came in simultaneously - pom-poms, shrapnel, 12-pdrs. and Maxims. We were and are completely surrounded ... We have only one gun, a 7-pdr., which is almost useless against the opposing guns with a superior range and we have only a few shells.'

Thirty-two casualties were sustained that day. One, a fatal one, was Corporal Norton, whose trench was not much use. The stone with its jolly message was, later, turned on end to form his gravestone. Carrington's column came within view of the Post by the afternoon, and came under Boer shellfire. It withdrew 17 miles (27km) to Marico River. The next day Baden-Powell marched from Rustenburg for Elands River, but assumed the fading sound of gunfire indicated Carrington's success and turned back. The Boers continued to shell the Australians.

On Wednesday 8 August a shell hit the hospital which was flying a Red Cross flag. Later that day a message under flag of truce was delivered by a ZARP lieutenant, and the opportunity was taken to protest about the hospital. The next day De la Rey sent to propose surrender, which Hore declined to do. Friday and Saturday saw fierce fighting over the water supply, but the Boers were beaten off. Sometime early in the next week a message from De la Rey to De Wet, who had crossed the Vaal a few days earlier, was intercepted by Lord Kitchener's columns. It immediately became clear that the men at Elands River, far from having surrendered, were still fighting. Kitchener at once set out to relieve them and, aware of his approach, the Boers faded away. Lance-corporal O. F. H. Middleton, New South Wales Citizens' Bushmen wrote:

'We had great forts at Elands River. When Kitchener arrived we were all underground. We used to camp in the forts with one man on watch, and as soon as the flash of a big gun was seen we all used to get underground quite safe. All the Lords and Generals with Kitchener said it was wonderful how we held out ... that it was one of the grandest things of the war.'

ROBERTS'S FINAL BLOW

East of Pretoria the two British armies were in contact by 15 August when elements of French's cavalry and

Buller's men met at Twyfelaar, some 30 miles (50km) south-east of Middleburg. There Buller was ordered to stay for the time being. On the hills east of Middleburg Botha had taken position on a line five miles (8km) east of Belfast with protection for his flanks anchored on Lydenburg and Barberton. The terrain either side of the railway was difficult, boggy to the south and mountainous to the north, so exotic outflanking movements were not possible.

Deneys Reitz, with the Pretoria commando, had been falling back from the capital in July and August.

'... great numbers of troops ... moved to right and left of the railway, sweeping us easily before them... In this manner we retreated for four or five days, by which time the English had pushed us along the railway line, through the town of Middleburg, and right up to Belfast village ... we were allotted a position on the edge of the escarpment near Machadodorp, where General Botha intended making a stand athwart the Delagoa railway. Along this crest he was going to fight a last pitched battle before taking to guerilla war.'

On 25 August French moved against the Boer right north of the railway while Pole-Carew faced the right centre and Buller, south of the railway, took on the left, where young Reitz was positioned with the Johannesberg ZARPs near Bergendal farm to the right of his Pretorian comrades. British shelling was ferocious. Reitz wrote:

'By ten [am] a heavy bombardment was in full swing,

Above **A staff officer receives a report from a private of the Royal Canadian Regiment while a trooper of Rimington's Scouts considers a possible conquest.**

(Gerry Embleton, from Men-at-Arms 303 *Boer Wars (2) 1898–1902*)

Right **The ZARP Memorial at Bergendal.** (M&CF)

although no actual advance was attempted, as they evidently intended first to batter down our works. This lasted until sunset … Next day the programme was repeated. We were shelled to such an extent that one dared scarcely look over the edge of the breastworks … Several of our men were wounded, and my brother Hjalmar was shot below the eye…

'*In the afternoon a detachment of infantry came down a defile on our left. We saw them in time to drive them back, killing and wounding about fifteen … As soon as it grew light on the third day, the bombardment recommenced more furiously than ever, but, instead of being spread all over our front, it was concentrated on that section held by the Johannesburg Police, a mile to our right.*'

The weight of shell battering the unfortunate ZARPs was immense, but when the 2nd Rifle Brigade on the left and the 1st Inniskillings on the right, advancing in short bounds from cover to cover, came near plenty of the Boers were alive to open fire. Mauser and pom-pom were brought to bear on them and the Inniskillings, replacements for the fallen of Hart's Hill, hesitated before gathering themselves to keep pace with the Rifles in a final bayonet charge. The bravery of the ZARPs was outstanding but fruitless; as a formation they ceased to exist.

Left **In the building of the new memorial to the ZARP, the exisiting memorial to the Rifle Brigade's fallen at Bergendal was moved and renovated.** (M&CF)

Below **A lone replica Creusot stands guard at Long Tom Pass, Rhenosterhoek, facing the eastern slope of the Mauchsberg, the route of the British advance from Lydenburg.** (M&CF)

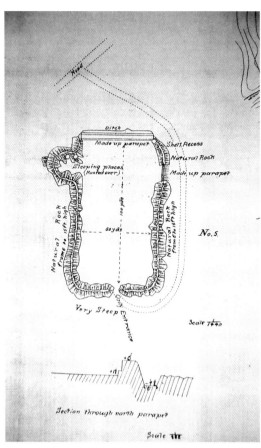

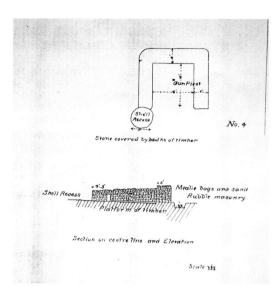

Left **Details of gun emplacements (GE) and gun pits (GP) from the map of Boer positions. Numbers 1,2 and 3 were next to the railway, 4 and 5 top right.**

(BL E54:13 [37])

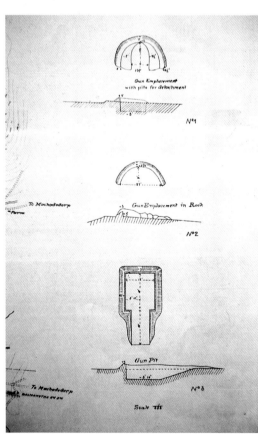

From the postion gained the British could enfilade the Boer line. It could not hold. Reitz and his comrades had been watching, unable to intervene.

'By sunset the police were all but annihilated, and in the dusk we saw the English infantry break into their positions. Here and there a hunted man went running down the slope behind, but the majority of the defenders were killed. Our line being broken, we had to give way too, and after dark General Botha ordered a withdrawal.'

The Boer force fell back, many rushing towards Komati Poort and leaving for Europe, President Kruger eventually among them. Those remaining split up into smaller units and scattered to the north, making their way through the hills, some for home, others to continue the fight. On 1 September Buller moved from Helvetia towards Lydenburg in pursuit of Botha. He soon ran into the Boer rearguard which opened fire with Creusot and pom-pom, closing the way forward through this mountainous country. Ian

Hamilton moved towards Dullstroom to threaten the Boer flank and Buller's opponents faded away. Both columns entered Lydenburg on 7 September and immediately came under fire from a Long Tom on the Spitzkop (Sabie) road. This ridge-top road was taken the next day and on Buller pressed. The fight resumed on the Devil's Knuckles and it was not until 27 September that the British finally came to Pilgrim's Rest, the end of the road for the Natal Army.

Sir Redvers Buller returned to England early in October and Lord Roberts was not long in following him. Clearly, the war was won, except for some tidying up which Roberts was happy to leave to Kitchener. The tiny bands of stubborn fighters could not long survive, especially now that their support system, the farms of family and friends, were being burnt and their last supply line, the eastern railway, was lost to them. It was obvious, logical. It was mistaken.

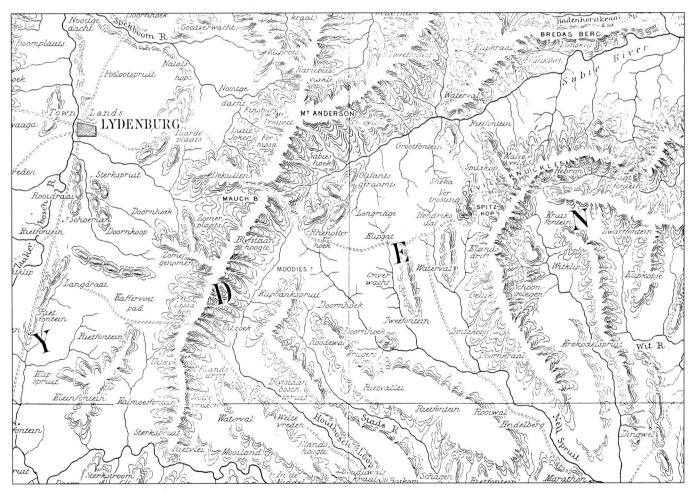

Left **Detail from a map made in August 1900 of the Boer positions at Belfast. Bergendal Farm is south of the railway in the centre, with trenches made at the Spring and, to the right, in two lines shown by dots running south-east below the place name. The main entrenchments are north of the farm and the railway, ending at the gun emplacement 'GE'. There are further gun emplacements on the railway to the east, and at the extreme north-east a laager.** (BL E54:13[37])

TOTAL WAR

To carry on the war the Boers depended on their ability to operate without massive supply-wagon trains such as those that had burdened, and contributed to the defeat of, Cronje and Prinsloo. Of necessity lightly armed and without heavy artillery, guerilla tactics were mandatory, though it should be noted that De Wet renounced the word 'guerilla', probably attributing to it a taint of unlawfulness. Strategically, what could be achieved with such tactics was limited. Attacks on targets of opportunity could irritate, but not destroy, the British. Blowing up railway bridges and ripping up lines could hamper, but not defeat, them. The only possibility of victory appears to have been seen as

making the British so fed up with the whole business that they would go away, to continue inflicting petty loss on petty loss until the will to persist had vanished and a peace favourable to the Boers could be negotiated. It was decided to add to the guerilla operations within the annexed republics new forays into the British colonies in order to foment uprisings by the Afrikaners. The British problem is easier to express but was extremely difficult to solve; how to pin down and kill or capture these roving commandos.

The experience of August in the Magaliesberg illustrated the point. De Wet crossed the Vaal to join De la Rey early in August 1900, having made his way

Below **A derailed train north of Dannhauser station, 21 August 1900.** (McM. MFME BW11/25)

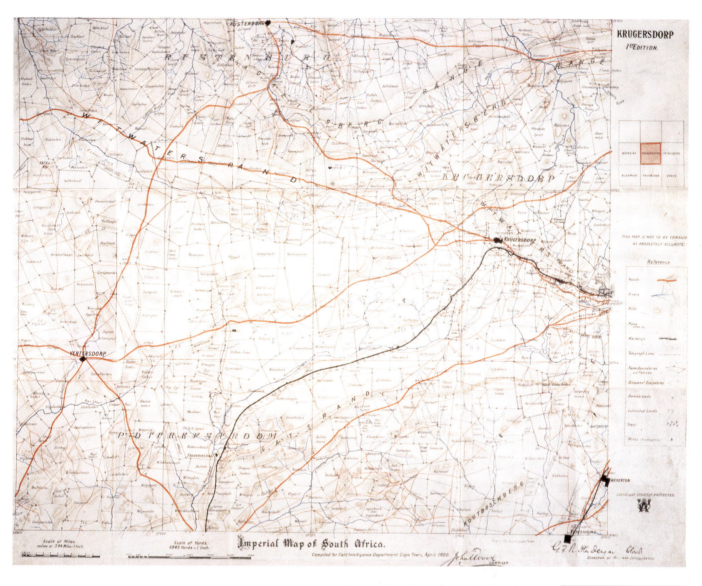

Imperial Map of South Africa.

Compiled for Field Intelligence Department, Cape Town, April, 1900.

across the Orange Free State from the Brandwater Valley pursued by Brigadier-general C. P. Ridley's 2nd Mounted Infantry Brigade and its numerous Australians. It was on 19 July, during this flight to the west, that Piet De Wet met his brother at Paardenkraal, 10 miles (16km) north-east of Kroonstadt, and received short shrift when he raised the question of making peace. If the two men met again Christiaan makes no mention of it. Piet rode off to accept the British offer of amnesty. As De Wet approached the Vaal the New South Wales Mounted Rifles, Kitchener's Horse and some Imperial Bushmen captured six wagons of his supplies at Klipstapel. In the counter-attack De Wet lost five killed and 12 wounded and the colonials lost two killed and 33 wounded. Here Captain Neville Howse of the New South Wales Army Medical Corps won Australia's first Victoria Cross for rescuing a young trumpeter under fire. Such was the pressure this side of the Vaal that De Wet decided to cross. Methuen's men, however, were

Above **The Krugersdorp sheet of a set of maps compiled for Field Intelligence Department, Cape Town and printed there, April 1900. Rustenburg is at the top of the sheet with the Magaliesberg Range immediately below with the road, in red, running through Olifant's Nek. Johannesburg is on the extreme right, mostly off the map, and Vereeniging in the bottom right corner.** (NAM86822)

Left **Captain Ripley, 2nd Northamptons, takes a rest.** (NRA. MFME BW1/4)

on the move on the far bank, among them young Barton with the Northamptons. On 6 August he noted that De Wet had been reported in the vicinity, and over the next few days the Northamptons slogged along in the wake of the mounted infantry. He says Methuen's Division had engaged the elusive Boer the next day at Tijgerfontein, near Venterskroon, but the Northamptons saw none of it. They were marching from Forsmans Drift and did not complete the 10 miles (16km) until 11am, by which time the Boers

had withdrawn in the face of artillery fire and the attacks of the Scots and Welsh Fusiliers. Barton wrote:

'The Boers as usual fled precipitately from the heavy artillery fire in spite of the fact that the country all round is hilly & almost mountainous. If held by determined men … a force 4 or 5 times that of the defenders would be unable to get through but the Boers are now short of guns and ammunition… De Wet in magnificent country for resistance was routed & driven back across the Vaal …'

In this he was mistaken. De Wet withdrew, but to march north and that evening he blew a bridge and broke the railway line north of Frederickstad, and, joining forces with Liebenberg's commando on the Mooi River, pushed on towards Ventersdorp. The British were hot on his heels. De Wet said:

'It was impossible to think of fighting - the enemy's numbers were far too great. Our only safety lay in flight. We knew very well that an Englishman cannot keep up with a Boer on the march, and that if he tries to do so, he soon finds that his horses and oxen can go no further. Our intention was then to march at the very best pace we could … Nevertheless we had to do some fighting …'

The pursuing British came on as swiftly as possible. On 9 August the Northamptons had already marched 8 miles (13km) and halted for food at 10.30am when:

'We had hardly settled down when the report came in that De Wet's laager had been located some 2 miles off. Soon Yeomanry & guns were off in hot haste & soon the guns were heard getting to work. At the same time two of

Below **The Kettering Men. A group of friends from Kettering joined the 1st Volunteer Battalion, the Northamptonshire Regiment together. All except one, Private J. B. Cooper, returned safely. A number of them had this photo taken by a Boer prisoner at Worcester in April 1901. From left to right and from back to front they are: A. L. Bird, W. Warrender, J. C. Crouch, F. Iliffe and W. Essam; F. Ireson, G. E. Lygo, W. Dobson, Frank Everett, D. Jackson and T. Gray; G. Northern and G. Martin.** (NRA. MFME BW2/1)

our ox convoy wagons were set alight by a grass fire … [we] hurried after the yeomanry. We must have done two hours without a halt at about 4 miles an hour [6.4km/hr]. In the distance we could see our shells bursting among the hills … soon the grass was blazing in all directions then the guns & yeomanry rushed out of sight.'

De Wet was obliged to sacrifice one of his Krupp 75mm guns to cover his retreat and to let his prisoners go. He also fired the Veldt to destroy the pasturage. On he marched, by night if needful, striking north for the Magaliesberg range. Meanwhile Kitchener had telegraphed Roberts to ask for Hamilton to move westwards from Commando Nek, on the Rustenburg to Pretoria road, to cut De Wet off before he could escape through Oliphant's Nek, from which the British had only just been withdrawn. Hamilton took the slower route south of the Magaliesbergs and arrived there on the evening of 14 August. De Wet had passed over it earlier that afternoon. Kitchener himself was now moving further west to relieve the Australians at Elands River Post and the pursuit of De Wet was abandoned. Within a week he had slipped back over the Magaliesbergs, taking an unmapped route over the hills and moving back to the Free State. On the way he met Danie Theron for the last time, for the scout was to lose his life shortly thereafter when the British caught him in a fight in the Gatsrand hills.

By the end of September Roberts had to recognise that De Wet was succeeding in bringing apparently

amnestied Boers back into the field against him. The response was to proclaim that the farms of such people would be burnt. The sympathies of the British troops were not with the Boers in this, upsetting though they generally found it to turn women and children out of their homes and set the buildings on fire. Captain H. H. Brown of the Imperial Bushmen wrote on 28 August:

'During the last few days a new proclamation has been issued, warning the Boer that their property will be

Right **Only rarely was swift entrenchment possible in the rocky terrain. Here British troops hurry to build sangars.** (McM. MFME BW16/7)

Below **Kritzinger's Commando in Cape Colony.** (McM. MFME BW11/37)

destroyed if they are found in arms … The Boer women light the signal fires and send due notice of our presence… In my opinion the only way of speedily terminating the war is to declare the whole district, when they are found in arms, as rebel districts, destroy the farms and commandeer the cattle. The want of supplies would speedily bring them into submission.'

De Wet argued that, having sworn their oath of neutrality and been promised protection by the British, the protection, far from being given, was actually needed against the depredations of the British themselves. But the logic of this is spoiled when he continues to suggest that, because some 'neutral' Boers began to fight on the English side, all others were released from their undertakings, that no Government, i.e. De Wet representing the former Free State government, need acknowledge an oath their citizens had no right to take and, finally, that to fight against the British was an obligation of anyone not a coward. This incoherent portfolio of justifications gave expression to a simple sentiment: the British are the enemy and a Boer's duty is to fight them. He therefore felt justified in treating the 'hands-uppers' as traitors, and their freedom and property as forfeit.

SOUTH FROM BELFAST

Major-general Horace Smith-Dorrien was sent to Belfast in October to assume command of the forces already in place, including Canadian Mounted Rifles and Royal Canadian Dragoons units, bringing with him more Dragoons, Gordon Highlanders and King's Shropshire Light Infantry. The operations of early November illustrated once more the errors of the British approach. Smith-Dorrien wanted to establish control of the country to the south and east, towards Carolina and the Komati River. The effort, started on 1 November, petered out in rainstorms which made bivouacking misery and hampered movement. On 6 November a more robust foray was undertaken in better weather and the advanced troops under Lieutenant-colonel Lessard, Canadian Mounted

Rifles, pushed the Boers back over successive ridges on the road to and beyond Van Wyks Vlei. From the high ground of Witkloof overlooking the Komati River they could see a line of trees and a low kopje between them and the river. A sharp fight developed with the Boers under cover of those features and it lasted until the afternoon when the Boers' left was threatened and they withdrew. Overnight Smith-Dorrien decided to withdraw to Belfast once more as the cost of what little success he had enjoyed was high. The Boers, under Generals J. C. Fourie and H. Grobler and Commandant H. R. Prinsloo, assumed the British would continue their advance and planned to attack them when they were extended by the process of crossing the river.

In the event the flexibility and mobility of the Boers nearly ruined Smith-Dorrien's retreat. As the cumbersome baggage train rumbled north once more the Boers sought to envelop the flanks of the column. Smith-Dorrien sent Lieutenant-colonel T. D. B. Evans, Canadian Mounted Rifles, with 35 men to sieze the kopje the Boers had defended the day before, and Fourie raced him for it. The Canadians won, and Lessard was able to keep the rearguard moving, the guns of D Battery, Royal Canadian Field Artillery leapfrogging back, laying down covering shrapnel turn and turn about. The Colt machine-gun of Sergeant E. J. Holland was also busy. As they continued to withdraw to Leliefontein, pressure on the flanks was resisted but the centre was allowed to become weaker and the Boers exploited the opportunity and Evans, who had left the kopje, was sent back to cover the dragoons. Fourie decided to make a thrust in the centre to capture the guns and, together with Prinsloo, died in the attempt. The Colt jammed. Holland dismounted it and staggered with the burning hot weapon to one of the gun limbers to deny it to the Boers. Isolated parties of Canadians were obliged to surrender, but they got the guns away and the withdrawal as a whole was secured. Three Victoria Crosses were awarded to Canadians for their actions on 7 November. It was clear that the British had much to learn.

A CLOSE CALL FOR DE WET

Early in November President Steyn and Christiaan De Wet met near Ventersdorp, north of Potchefstroom, and moved south to Bothaville in the north-western Free State. Steyn wanted to accompany De Wet on a raid into Cape Colony and the decision required discussion with leaders of other groups. On 5 November they met General Froneman at Bothaville on the Valsch River, a smart skirmish making them aware of a British presence on the north bank of the stream. De Wet set look-outs to keep an eye on them.

Soon after dawn the next day Lieutenant-colonel P. W. J. Le Gallais with the 5th and 8th Mounted

Infantry attacked. The Boers were, for once, taken entirely by surprise. De Wet wrote:

'The scene which ensued was unlike anything I had witnessed before… Whilst I was looking for my horse to get him up-saddled a few of the burghers were making some sort of stand against the enemy. But all those who had already up-saddled were riding away at break-neck speed. Many were even leaving their saddles behind and galloping off bare-back.'

There was nothing De Wet could do to stop the rot. Steyn escaped, as did De Wet, and the only resistance came from a little group of Boers who were unable to ride off. They occupied a small farm house and exchanged fire with the British who had taken another farm some 200 yards (180m) away. The fight continued for four hours while Major-general Charles Knox's column made its leisurely approach. Le Gallais was fatally wounded. Of him De Wet wrote: 'The leader of the enemy's storming party was Colonel Le Gallais, without doubt one of the bravest English officers I have ever met.'

The Boers lost between nine (De Wet) and 25 (British report) killed, and some 30 wounded and over 100 taken prisoner. All their guns, four 75mm, one of the Colenso 15-pdrs. and a 12-pdr. from Sannaspos, were lost to them, though De Wet claimed they were almost out of ammunition so it did not matter. The scattering burghers were allowed to escape.

De Wet made his way south, taking the town of his youth, Dewetsdorp, named after his father, and then attempting to enter Cape Colony, a scheme in which he was foiled. The distraction this caused enabled two groups, one under Herzog and the other commanded by Kritzinger, to enter the colony and

Above **On 12 November 1900 Lieutenant Barton was touched by a gift of flowers from a little girl in Ventersdorp. Her father, she told him, had been away a long time and was at Green Point. That was a prisoner of war camp. All Barton could do was assure her that her father would be well looked after and properly fed. The flowers were kept in the journal.** (NRA. MFME BW17/28 or 17/29)

Above **De Wet's Commando crosses the Orange River.**
(McM. MFME BW12/2)

threaten the security of the railways through De Aar and Naauwpoort.

NOOITGEDACHT

Lord Roberts left South Africa at the end of November to enjoy a triumphant return to England, leaving Kitchener as C-in-C. The start of his command was not a happy one. Major-general R. A. P. Clements was camped on the supply route to Rustenburg which ran along the valley between the Magaliesbergs and the Witwatersberg at a place called Nooitgedacht where a fresh stream provided all the clear water he could desire and a mountain-top post permitted heliograph communication with General Broadwood in Rustenburg. The position was also about as vulnerable as could be to a determined assault. On the morning of 13 December the Boers attacked.

Deneys Reitz was with General Beyers, with whom the Afrikander Cavalry Corps was now serving. Beyers and De la Rey had some 1,500 men, half as many again as Clements's force, and devised a plan to overcome the British. Beyers's men would take the high ground, some 1,000 feet (300m) above the valley floor along which De la Rey would attack, also from the west. Beyers's men made a night approach, Reitz recounts.

'Towards morning, tired and sleepy, we halted for an hour ... General Beyers, whatever his faults, was a bold and resourceful leader and he made immediate preparations for the assault. Ordering all horses to be left behind, he passed word we were to advance on foot... We of the "A.C.C." were on the extreme right at the edge of the cliff ... Before we had gone far dawn lit the mountain-tops, and with it came a fierce rifle-fire from the enemy schanses some distance ahead.'

The Boers were worn out with travel and lack of sleep and went to ground immediately. Nothing Beyers could do would get them moving again. Then, as they looked down on the British camp below, De la Rey's men came galloping in on it, only to recoil before the answering fire. Opposite Reitz the Northumberland Fusiliers burst into loud cheers, thus stimulating Beyers's commandos to action their general had failed to inspire. They rose and charged the British! Reitz again:

'There was no stopping us now, and we swept on shouting and yelling, men dropping freely as we went. Almost before we knew it, we were swarming over the walls, shooting and clubbing in hand-to-hand conflict. It was sharp work. I have a confused recollection of fending bayonet thrusts and firing point-blank into men's faces; then of soldiers running to the rear or putting up their hands, and as we stood panting and excited within the barricades, we could scarcely realize that the fight was won.'

Lieutenant Jack Gilmour of 20th Company (Fife and Forfar), Imperial Yeomanry wrote to his mother from Reitfontein on 14 December:

'Yesterday at 4am we were wakened by very heavy firing … An hour later we had all our horses in the bottom of the kloof [ravine] as bullets were dropping into Camp and killed two mules. We heard very heavy firing on the hill … Robin Purvis and Campbell with all available men, and all the Devons under Captain Bolitho and Lt. Eaton were sent up to reinforce the Northumberlands. Before these got up, the Boers … had taken the hill tops and our men met the Fusiliers coming down pell mell. Poor Robin was shot down at once … they are all prisoners - twenty-six men and two officers, and all the Devons and their Officers.'

Reitz, while looking for a source of water to give the wounded a drink, came across the men coming up from the British camp and called for help to stop them.

'… We ran down just in time to see the path crowded with soldiers. We lost no time in pouring close-range volleys into their midst. In less than a minute only dead and wounded were left … In passing by the intake of the gorge, I found the soldier whom I had killed. I was horrified to see that my bullet had blown half his head away, the explanation being that during one of our patrols near the Warm Baths I had found a few explosive Mauser cartridges at a deserted trading station, and had taken them for shooting game. I kept them in a separate pocket of my bandolier, but in my excitement had rammed one of them into the magazine of my rifle without noticing it… there is not a great deal of difference between killing a man with an explosive bullet, and smashing him with a lyddite shell, although I would not knowingly have used this type of ammunition.'

From the mountain-top the Boers descended to ransack the British camp, to the fury of General Beyers who tried to make them follow up the retreating remains of Clements's force. Reitz and his companions reasoned that they had done their share, that acquiring supplies was sensible where taking prisoners was just a nuisance, and that De la Rey's men could finish what they had failed to achieve earlier in the day. As a result,

'We were refitted from head to heel, we carried a Lee-Metford rifle apiece, in lieu of our discarded Mausers, and above all we were well found in horse-flesh.'

Clements, having got his men into this fix,

proceeded to get them out of it. Orders were given for tents and baggage to be abandoned and the Yeomanry and Yorkshire Light Infantry to cover the withdrawal towards Reitfontein. The big gun, Gilmour calls it a 5in., other sources a 4.7in., ox-drawn, was a problem as many of the draft animals had been killed. With the gunners, Gilmour and his men worked to bring it back.

'All the niggers had bolted and left the oxen, Sergt. Pullar is a hero, and did A1… We worked away with the oxen under a heavy fire and at last got things more or less straight and so we were told to go. We retired under a very heavy fire … Horses, mules and men were being hit right and left and the whole place was in a ferment…

'I got back and was ordered to take all available Yeomanry and hold a position for the guns… We worked for dear life building sangars, and I helped the Gunners to pull the gun into position. We then shelled I fear both friend and foe, there was no other way. Then the Boers shelled us …'

They had contrived to take up position on a hill, called Yeomanry Hill by the British, south of the river at Hartebeestfontein and from here were able to halt the Boer advance. Some 200 men ran, together with the wagons, a panic that was stopped and, indeed reversed when soldiers returned to cover the withdrawal. Gilmour again:

'I then reinforced Sir Elliot Lees and held a kopje to cover the retirement of what was left of our Brigade. I am told we lost 650 men killed, wounded and prisoners. We retired at 4pm, and we fought our way back until dark. It was hot work and few of us will ever forget it.'

CLEARING THE LAND

The dawn of a new year brought little encouragement to the British. It seemed to them that peace was possible if only they could start talking to the Boers and if the Boers would be reasonable. Attempts to send surrendered burghers as emissaries resulted in those unfortunates being executed as traitors but, eventually, Kitchener managed to enlist the aid of the widow of General Joubert in getting a message to Louis Botha. That gained only the answer that they were fighting for their independence. The two men finally met on February 28, when Kitchener proposed that, while the annexation of the republics was irreversible, it could be agreed that the position of the native population would be unchanged, the Boers would be full citizens, that war damage would be compensated and that all, including rebel citizens of the British colonies, would be granted amnesty. The British government failed to support Kitchener's ideas, first on the amnesty question and second on the treatment of 'Kaffirs' whose rights, it was said, should be at least equal to those prevailing in Cape Colony. No agreement could be reached and the war continued with De Wet making a grand foray into Cape Colony.

In spite of the greatest efforts, the British failed to catch him. For two weeks De Wet's column swept round, chased and harried but still free until, finally, it crossed back over the Orange River. Nothing of value accrued to the Boers other than romantic publicity. Those Cape rebels that joined him, or other commandos, and were subsequently caught were treated as traitors by the British; many of them were hanged.

The British problem, however, persisted. The Boers were still in the field and it was necessary to maintain a huge force to guard the railways and bridges against their attacks and until something new was done this would just go on. The plan to put an end to the marauding commandos was simple in concept. They would be driven like game into a corral of British troops and their support in the field, the farms and their inhabitants, taken from them. The country would be cleared of both active and passive resistance. In order to achieve this the British would build, over the next year or so, a network of blockhouses and fortified railway stations to fence in the commandos. They would mount great drives across miles of Veldt to sweep up the Boers. They would destroy the farms, but, in order to avoid harm to non-combatants, they would accommodate the refugees in camps.

THE FORTIFICATIONS

The building of blockhouses had started in March 1900 to protect the railways, and in particular the railway bridges. Impressive structures of stone arose, with corrugated iron roofs, standing three storeys high and entered, like medieval keep towers, by an external wooden stair which could be withdrawn. Lieutenant Barton visited one:

'... a tower some 35ft [10.6m] high, loopholed with iron plates let into the masonry. The entrance by means of a ladder which can be drawn up into the centre story. A trap door in the floor of which leads down into the basement also loopholed, another ladder & trap door leads up to the top story also loopholed from which jut out two iron plates machicoli galleries or balconies whence flanking fire can be delivered, loopholes in the floor of these enable men to fire perpendicularly down on attackers below ... Holding about 24 men these towers are practically impregnable against Boers only armed with rifles. However we shall not end the war by sitting still in them.'

Although very effective, such sophisticated forts were both expensive and time-consuming to build. A more modest structure was a rectangular, single-storey affair with a stone wall surmounted by a corrugated iron upperwork, pierced with loopholes and double skinned, the space between the layers being filled with stones to exclude rifle fire. Even this was too slow in the construction and, for the serious mass-production of blockhouses needed to create effective barriers across the huge distances of the Veldt, Kitchener turned to Major Spring R. Rice, Officer Commanding 23 Field Company, Royal Engineers at Middleburg, Transvaal.

Rice designed two blockhouses, one octagonal and the other, the one that has become known as the

'Rice Blockhouse', circular. It was made of corrugated iron with a stone-filled, loopholed shield above and an earth-filled caisson below, the whole topped off with a stout roof. When ideally sited the door was approached under cover of a trench and the hillock on which it sat and the lower part of the walls covered with loose stones for added protection. Trained men could, it is said, erect such a blockhouse in a single day and the record for building one was a mere three hours. It was usually garrisoned by a non-commissioned officer and six men. Outside the immediate area was protected by barbed wire and a barbed wire fence stretched between one blockhouse and the next, hung about with tin cans to make as much noise as possible when disturbed.

The fortifications included numerous other models, often ad-hoc designs fashioned to meet the requirements of the location and adjusted to make the best of available materials, but the Rice design was the

Above **A very substantial tower photographed by Ronald C. Delany of 33rd IY. It was, he states, protecting the bridge over the Kaffir River.** (TM. MFME BW3/5)

Right **A picture of Lieutenant Barton in the process of building a blockhouse at Wagonboom Poort in September 1901. He has kindly shown which one he is with the letter B.** (NRA. MFME BW1/14)

Above **A rectangular blockhouse in Ladysmith.** (McM. MFME BW11/8)

Left **A Rice blockhouse within a barbed wire defence work, photographed by Major G. N. M. Darwell.** (NRA. MFME BW1/36)

Right **The replica blockhouse built as a museum by Doug McMaster near Ladysmith.** (MFME BW7/6)

Below **A drawing of a Rice blockhouse by Captain R. E. Harvey, RE dated 19 April 1902.** (RE7406.03. MFME BW19/6)

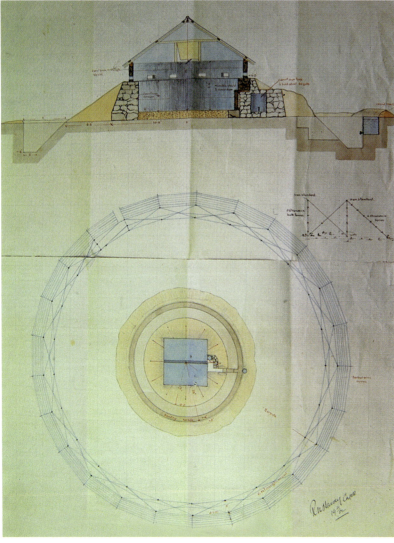

Right **Drawing No. 338d, of a 'Rice' blockhouse.** (RE5201.34.1. MFME BW18/34)

Centre right **Drawing No. 336 of a hexagonal timber roof for a blockhouse to be built at French Hoek Pass.** (RE5201.34.1. MFME BW18/39)

Below right **The Orange River Station blockhouse still stands, untouched for a century.** (MFME BW13/5)

Below **At the War Museum of the Boer Republics in Bloemfontein a replica Rice blockhouse stands near a locomotive, built in Glasgow in 1893, which saw service in the war.** (MFME BW14/37)

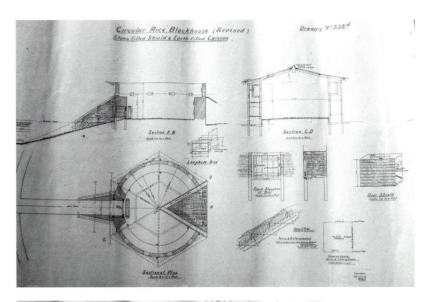

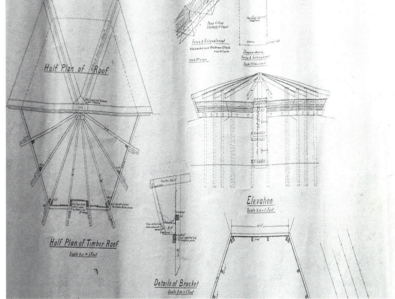

one that sprang up in huge numbers. By September 1901 the Western Railway blockhouse line from De Aar to Lobatsi, north of Mafeking, was complete, as was the Central Railway system from Naauwpoort to Pretoria and the Delagoa Railway to the border at Koomati Poort. In addition a box west of Johannesburg and Pretoria and a line south-east to Standerton and Newcastle were operational. In the next three months the line north from Pretoria to Pietersberg was built, the Western Railway cover

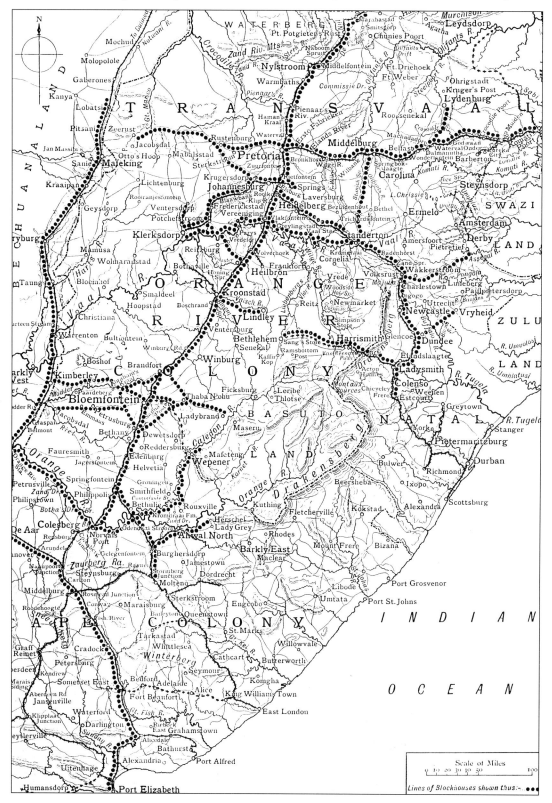

Left Map of the blockhouse lines as completed in 1901 from *After Pretoria: The Guerilla War*.

Right Part of a plan, undated, of the Pretoria to Pietersburg railway north of Nylstroom, the country in which the Gordon Highlanders were ambushed. (RE9301.15/16. MFME BW19/9)

Below right Work in progress at Naboomspruit (see pp. 142-143). A photograph from the water tower, from which engines were replenished, looking south-west showing the building of the shelter 'S' and the barbed wire enclosure. The blockhouse has not been started. (NRA MFME BW1/28)

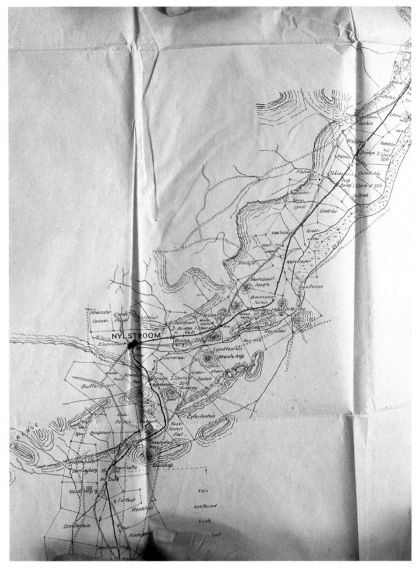

were quickly killed or mortally wounded and all the rest hit. Dunlop Best was challenged to surrender, refused and was shot. It was further reported that the driver, fireman and guard were shot down in cold blood before the train was plundered and set on fire. Barton wrote of his last meeting with Best:

'... we had a chat while the engine watered, while we talked a scout came in & reported three Boer patrols of 5 each some five miles [8km] away in a direction almost at right angles to the railway ... I told Best of them & he laughed & said "I must get my gun loaded" & off he went, little did I think that I should next see him cold & stiff not only killed but stripped of boot & coat only his kilt & shirt left to him.'

Barton reports that the attacking Boers were under the command of Beyers, who intervened to halt the plundering of the wounded. He wrote:

'I always have sympathy with brave men fighting for their country, to attack & capture trains is part of warfare of course, but to murder unarmed men in cold blood & to outrage the wounded is the work not of soldiers but of Brigands & Bandits ... if the murderers could be found they should be left hanging on the trees near the place they committed it at.'

Barton had been alerted to the ambush by a runner carrying a message and immediately telegraphed for medical aid from Rust and reported to the OC Lines of Communication. Preparations were made to receive the wounded and a party sent downline under a white flag to retrieve them. The next day they turned their attention to the dead.

'... started parties digging the graves ... A most terrible sight that truck when we opened it. 15 bodies some bootless & coatless white & black fallen soldiers & murdered civilians the truck simply riddled with bullets. Some staring others gently smiling.'

extended south-west to Beaufort West and numerous additions made in Transvaal and what was now Orange Colony. By May 1902 a line of blockhouses ran from Beaufort West right across Cape Colony to the Atlantic coast and yet more lines had been added elsewhere. By the end of the war there were 3,700 miles (6,000km) of lines with some 8,000 blockhouses manned by 50,000 British troops and 16,000 Africans.

The 2nd Northamptonshire Regiment became involved with the protection of the railway line north from Pretoria. The kind of problem the Boers gave them was illustrated by the events of 4 July 1901. An armoured train on the way from Pretoria to Pietersburg was guarded by 28 men of the 2nd Gordon Highlanders under Lieutenant A. A. Dunlop Best. Soon after leaving Naboomspruit, where Best had had lunch with Lieutenant Barton earlier in the day, it was derailed by an explosion and attacked by a mounted band of Boers. Of the Gordons seven men

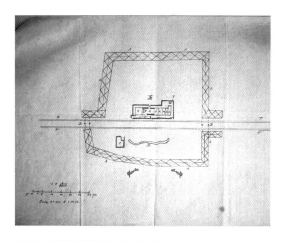

Above **The barbed wire enclosure. The station buildings are marked E, C is a rectangular blockhouse and D is a trench for emergencies. F is the main line and F' the siding. There are barbed wire gates at the two points marked B.**

Lieutenant Barton's record of the fortification of Naboomspruit Station. (NRA. MFME BW1/16 to 1/28)

Right **General layout. The station is enclosed with wire and the veldt has been cleared of trees for up to 800 yards (730m). The siding's junction with the main line is marked 'points' and the tanks outside the enclosure are for filling engines. The location of the demolished general store is shown.**

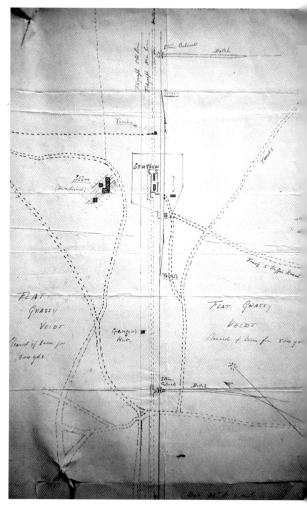

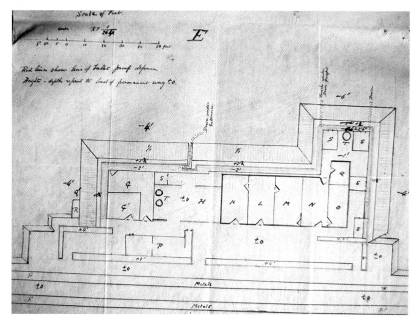

Above **The refreshment room and store, G and G', which became the telegraph office, were joined on to the rest of the station buildings to make a small fort. Water tanks are marked T and the various offices K to O. P is a loopholed shed for four men and two sappers and each of the shelters marked S is for two men.**

He read his first burial service over them on Saturday 6 July.

Between then and Barton's diary entry for 17 August the Boers tried the same trick. Barton reports:

'... the enemy having laid a self acting mine which exploded, stopping the train, they tried to get the protected truck of the escort, by firing a second with a string. A German doing this close to the line missed the truck, but ran forward calling out to the Gordons "Hands up". The Gordons put their rifles up instead.'

The Boers took cover and opened fire, but a second armoured train was close behind and opened up with shrapnel.

'The German string puller put up <u>his</u> hands & cried "Gentlemen I surrender" but the men of Best's regiment

remembering the 4th July were not inclined to give quarter & he with 6 others were buried close to the road crossing the rail, with an inscription designed in jam tins "Here lie 7 Train Wreckers."'

The war was turning yet uglier.

The centre of these activites, Naboomspruit Station, had been fortified by Barton during his three months there up to 9 July. The main building and the waiting room of the station were joined together and fortified as a combined blockhouse and headquarters building for a force to oversee the railway for some 17 miles (27km) north and south, over which African scouts patrolled between blockhouses. There was a blockhouse on the other side of the line from the main building, barbed wire defences and two large water tanks to reduce their dependence on outside supply. An area around the station was cleared. Saturday 25 May:

'The grass is so long & gives such good cover that I had always intended to burn it as soon as it was dry enough. Original plan being to have 200 yards [183m] round the building to graze cattle on.'

Two sergeants to whom the work was given proceeded to burn the area Barton wanted to keep for

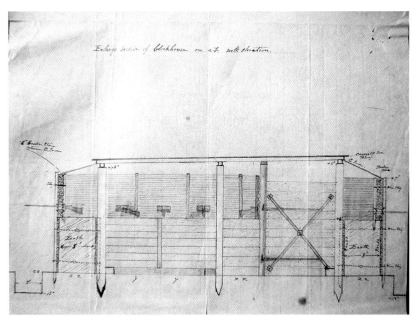

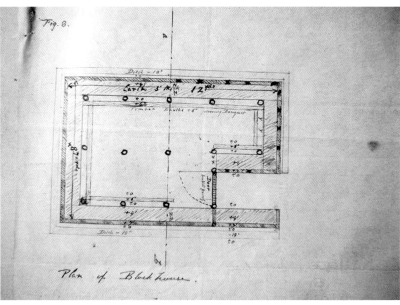

Above **The blockhouse in plan and in section on a/b.**

SWEEPS AND RAIDS

The first of Kitchener's sweeps to harvest the Boers yielded poor returns and inspired the blockhouse system. In the eastern Transvaal General French had eight columns comprised of some 22,000 men at his disposal, of whom two-thirds were combatants. In late January 1901 they had undertaken an operation to catch Botha, starting from lines running east from Pretoria and south from Johannesburg, each column advancing on a prescribed line to trap the prey against the Swaziland border and the Drakensbergs (see map on p. 144). The westerly columns moved off on 28 January and the north-easterly on 3 February. Ermelo was almost surrounded by 5 February and Botha was obliged to divide his forces, leaving about 1,500 men to cover the retreating families and taking 2,000 men to escape northwards. Deneys Reitz witnessed the British advance.

'As the sun rose, the sky-line from west to east was dotted with English horsemen riding in a line that stretched as far as the eye could see, and behind this screen every road was black with columns, guns, and wagons, slowly moving forward on the first great drive of the war... All that day we fell back, delaying the enemy horsemen by rifle-fire as far as possible ... During the course of the morning, pillars of smoke began to rise behind the English advance, and to our astonishment we saw that they were burning farmhouses as they came. Towards noon word spread that, not only were they destroying all before them, but were actually capturing and sending away the women and children. At first we could hardly credit this, but when one wild-eyed woman after another galloped by, it was borne in on us that a more terrible chapter of the war was opening.'

Smith-Dorrien's column was attacked and beat off the Boers, but the gaps between the columns were now large enough for Botha to retreat north instead of back into the swept area. The operation continued into April, but, with winter approaching, the gains were small. Only 1,332 Boers had been taken, either killed, captured or surrendered. Over a quarter of a million head of stock, sheep and cattle, had been acquired together with a great quantity of arms and ammunition, but the score in fighting men, the irreplaceable commodity for the Boers, was puny. What is more, their determination to fight was strengthened.

Reitz escaped the sweep and made his way back to the hills west of Johannesburg where De la Rey's forces were hiding and trekking to avoid the British. By the end of July he was moving towards the Orange River with a view to going to Cape Colony, falling in with small groups, remnants of once strong commandos, on the way. They were able to distract a British column attempting to round up a woman's laager, a band of refugees attempting to avoid internment in the camps and then spent some days trailing the British column

the cattle and leave the approaches to the station with ample cover. Barton remarked:

'All my best work has been done by Privates of the Reserve. N.C.O.s are willing enough but they lack ingenuity & common sense ... intellect[s] narrowed by the walls of the barrack square ...'

Barton was also faced with a polite enquiry from the owner of the local shop. The store had been flattened to give a field of fire and the materials incorporated in the new defences, while the furniture, according to Barton, had been smashed by Australian Bushmen. He passed the letter up to the O. C. Lines of Communication. Barton drew up precise plans for these works and even photographed the progress of the construction; another link in the chain of forts and lookouts that was being woven around the Boers.

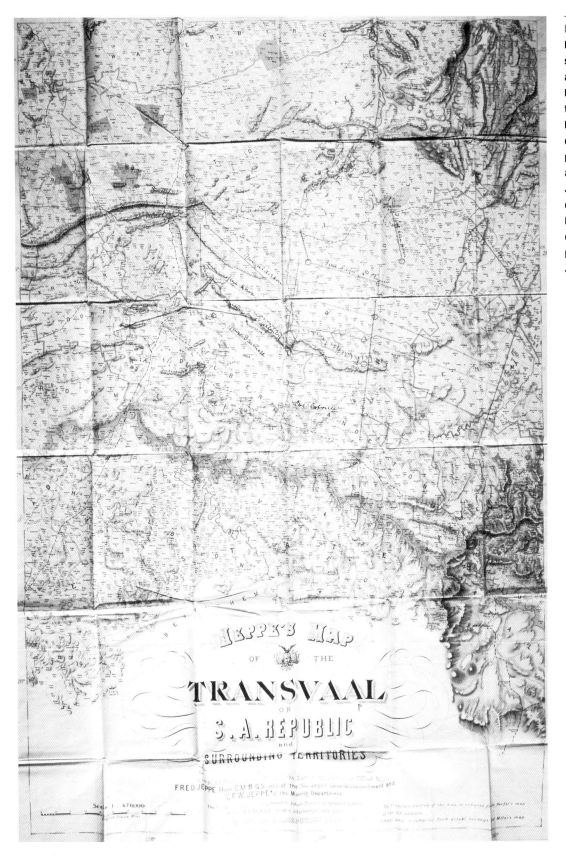

Left **A marked copy of Jeppe's Map of the Transvaal showing, left to right, axes of advance of the various units by commander and, vertically, the positions to be attained by a given date. The operation starts on a 27th, probably of January 1901, on a north-south line east of Johannesburg, and finishes on 6th & 7th, presumably February, involving eight columns. The map is from the papers of Lieutenant-colonel J. M. Grierson, AAG.** (NAM86823)

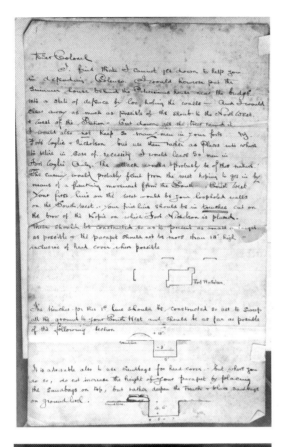

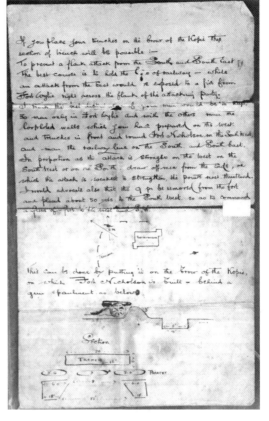

Left **A three page letter, signed R. Meyrick, and probably from Lieutenant Robert Evelyn Meyrick, RE, to an unknown colonel about the fortification of Colenso. He suggests putting the summer house behind the Policeman's house near the bridge into a state of defence and gives detailed advice on how to do it. Meyricke had distinguished himself by surveying the road bridge under fire at the Battle of Colenso and then served in Pietermaritzburg, where he died of enteric on 8 March 1900. This suggests that the fortification was being undertaken while the Boers were still in occupation of the hills north of the Tugela.**
(Graham Jacobsen Collection. Photo M. & C. French)

in order to collect .303 ammunition dropped by the careless soldiers. Thus re-supplied, they made for the river near Zastron. As they contemplated methods of crossing a large body of horsemen, Boer by their formation and behaviour, approached. It turned out to be Jan Smuts's force on its way to invade the Cape. They crossed successfully, lying low as a train passed in darkness along the Sterkstroom to Indwe branch line. It later emerged that General French was on that train. Then they narrowly escaped being caught by the 17th Lancers in the Stormberg Mountains, but they attacked with vigour and prevailed. Reitz was able to renew not only his arms and ammunition, but his entire wardrobe and acquire a new mount, at the expense of Lord Vivian who was wounded in the action. From there Smuts led them on a long ride of marauding first southwards and ultimately to the far north-west where they besieged O'Okiep. For nuisance value the expedition was a success and as a story of adventure, courage and excitement it is almost unrivalled. The only real contribution it made to the defeat of the British was to distract troops and attention from operations in the former republics.

The pattern of war now became one of raid and counter-raid. The British steadily gained in skill, depending increasingly on highly mobile columns under such commanders as Colonel G. E. Benson. The blockhouse lines closed down Boer movement significantly, even though De Wet spoke of the system

with contempt. But the Boers still refused to admit the hopelessness of their efforts. It remained to destroy their spirit, and that was done more by accident than design.

THE CAMPS

As the juggernaut of the British army rolled over the Veldt, burning farms and driving off cattle, the non-combatant population, both black and white, was swept up. Some evaded the soldiers and made off in their wagons with the servants and a few possessions, but the rest were looked after. Or that was the plan. Refugee camps were set up, under canvas, throughout

the land. Here the families who had surrendered or been captured were accommodated in the care, for the most part, of men who had no idea what to do. Indeed, the ignorance of the requirements of sanitation and the dangers of typhoid can be seen in its impact on the British army. Of some 22,000 British dead in this war, 62 per cent, about 13,500, died of disease. That the same organisation was not competent to run the so-called refugee camps is, though unforgivable, unsurprising.

Word had come to England of these camps and questions were being asked. In March 1901 two

Left **A rare survival, the graveyard at Doornbult, Orange River Station. The markers are made from tin cans and fixed with two nails to a stake. The white grave numbers have faded away. More than 230 people are buried here, 187 of them children.** (Photo Rina Wiid, Doornbult)

Below **A bird's-eye view of Norval's Pont, the crossing of the Orange River by the railway from Coleberg to Bloemfontein. The camp visited by Emily Hobhouse was 'far superior to the Camp at Bloemfontein. The spot chosen is a slope, surrounded by hills, about a mile from the station.' It had pure spring water and was not crowded.** (RE5201.34.2. MFME BW18/32)

members of Parliament spoke of them as 'concentration camps', after the *reconcentrado* camps established by the Spanish in Cuba. Information was squeezed from the Government; 21,105 people in Transvaal camps in April, 19,680 in Orange River Colony and 2,524 in Natal in May. The number of deaths was equally difficult to discover. Nor was it clear if the figures included the black inmates. The political pressure became so great because of the evidence gathered by Emily Hobhouse. She was funded by the Committee of the Distress Fund for South African Women and Children and arrived, with various supplies for the camps, in December 1900. She was granted permission to visit the camps by Sir Alfred Milner and Lord Kitchener. With a truck given

to her through Milner's good offices she set off for Bloemfontein with £200 worth of groceries and all the bales of clothing she could gather. On arrival at De Aar she happily set about unpacking and arranging her gifts. The expedition soon changed its character from the dispensation of comforts to the investigation of suffering on a scale that horrified her.

'The Bloemfontein Camp. January 26th. The exile *camp here is a good two miles from the town, dumped down on the southern slope of a kopje, right out on to the bare brown Veldt, not a vestige of a tree in any direction, nor shade of any description…*

'*Imagine the heat outside the tents, and the suffocation inside! We sat on their khaki blankets, rolled up, inside Mrs. B.'s tent; and the sun blazed through the*

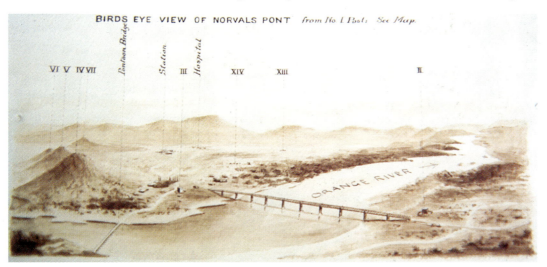

single canvas, and flies lay thick and black on everything; no chair, no table, nor any room for such; only a deal box, standing on its end, served as a wee pantry. In this tiny tent live Mrs. B.'s five children (three quite grown up) and a little Kaffir servant girl...

'Now I must tell you their rations:-
Daily -
Meat, ¹/₂lb (with bone and fat)
Coffee, 2oz.
Wholemeal, ³/₄lb.
Condensed milk, one-twelfth of tin.
Sugar, 2oz.
Salt, ¹/₂oz.
That is all, nothing else to fill in.

'January 31st... a girl of twenty-one lay dying on a stretcher. The father, a big, gentle Boer, kneeling beside her; while, next tent, his wife was watching a child of six, also dying, and one of about five drooping.'

Emily travelled to Norvals Pont and Aliwal North, Springfontein, Kimberley and Mafeking. She warned the readers of her report that each camp was different and conditions varied with the Commandant, the location and proximity of wood and water, the distance from a base and stores, the presence of public opinion and the date it was set up, for the older ones had been able to obtain items now no longer available. She was back in Bloemfontein on 22 April, when she reported that there were about 4,000 in the camp, double the number of six weeks before. The Springfontein camp had grown from 500 to 3,000 and, she wrote,

'... as we passed along yesterday morning there was a trainload in the station of 600 more. It was pitiable to see them - massed in the train, many of them in open trucks. It was bitterly cold ... Some women were pushing their way to the platform to try and buy food for their children. The soldiers would not permit this...

Left **The memorial to the dead at Howick, Natal. In spite of being set up next to the military hospital, the death rate in the camp was terrible. The top section of the panel records the names of the adults. The children are listed below.** (MFME BW2/8)

Right **Boer women and children being delivered to a camp.** (McG. MMKP7819/1 AND 7819/2)

Below **The Refugee Camp (sic) at Vluchteling.** (McG. MMKP5133)